# THE CARDINAL CLUB

# The Cardinal Club

*A Daughter's Journey to Acceptance*

A memoir
by

**SUZANNE MAGGIO**

Adelaide Books
New York / Lisbon
2019

THE CARDINAL CLUB
A memoir
By Suzanne Maggio

Copyright © by Suzanne Maggio
Cover design © 2019 Adelaide Books
Cover image by Suzanne Maggio


Published by Adelaide Books, New York / Lisbon
adelaidebooks.org
Editor-in-Chief
Stevan V. Nikolic

For any information, please address Adelaide Books
at info@adelaidebooks.org
or write to:
Adelaide Books
244 Fifth Ave. Suite D27
New York, NY, 10001


ISBN: 978-1-951214-87-6


Printed in the United States of America

*For my mother*

# Contents

# *Prologue*

Although I've spent more than thirty years helping families face the stories they could not face, I could not face my own.

It was the fall of 1991. I was a young social worker, married for five years and pregnant with my first child. While I tried to appear calm, my stomach was doing flip-flops, the way it so often did when I was about to speak my truth. I tugged at the blue cotton sundress that stretched across my growing belly and tightened my grip around the scroll of butcher paper that lay in my lap. *Was I ready to share my story?*

I'd signed up for an advanced seminar in family therapy and the instructor had assigned us the task of drawing our genogram. It is a tool used in therapy, a visual image that illustrates the people and connections in a family. It is used to help families share their history. This was the second time I'd done such an exercise. The first was early on in my social work career, when I was in graduate school, newly married and still struggling to find my way in the world. Strangely, few things had changed since then. Five years later, most of my grandparents were still alive. My brother and his wife had two children, but not much else was different. I drew double lines to indicate the strong relationship connections between my parents, grandparents and various sets of aunts and uncles. My grandmother

Maggio had been diagnosed with cancer a few years earlier, but most of the other members were healthy. I scribbled the word "Italian" above both families in bold letters.

My colleagues introduced us to their mothers and fathers, brothers, sisters and grandparents. On the surface, the genogram drawing seemed simple enough. A series of circles and squares, straight lines and broken ones. But images can be deceiving. It was behind the symbols that the richness lay. Stories of first dates, marriage and subsequent divorce. Alcohol abuse, addiction and a struggle to recover. One of my classmates grew up an only child. Another, his family with barely enough to eat. Still another emigrated from Mexico. You could barely hear a pin drop as she told the story of the *coyote* who guided her family across the border.

As we went around the room and shared our stories, a knot began to form in the pit of my stomach. I compared myself to the others. I'd grown up in a middle class family. My parents were still married. We always had enough food and I'd had the best education they could offer. I took tennis lessons and piano lessons and spent summers on vacation. There was no doubt I'd lived a privileged life. I felt lucky to have been given so much and I was grateful for all of it. Still, the pain my classmates shared lent a richness to their experience, a depth I longed for. I found myself embarrassed, as though the financially abundant life I'd led disqualified me in some way.

I needn't have worried. Although I couldn't see it at the time, I too had my own share of pain. Hidden behind the almost perfect façade was a truth my family would not allow and did not recognize. Facing the whole of my own life would give me all the lessons I would need. Clearly, I didn't know what I didn't know.

Over the years I have been challenged by my tendency to see only what I wanted to see. I was taught to be grateful for what I had. To focus on what is comfortable. It wasn't easy to say the unpopular thing, to stand alone in my truth. Like most of us, I wanted to be liked. To be accepted. In my own family I'd often chosen to apply a thick layer of whitewash to cover over the deep cracks and sharp edges, to ignore the hardships, the strife and the difficult relationships. The truth was, there *were* plenty of good things to focus on and I had been taught to appreciate them all. But ignoring the difficulties can make the good things seem shallow and the experience feel like a lie.

When my brothers, sister and I were children, my parents would take an annual Christmas card photo. On a fall day in late October, when the leaves were just beginning to turn orange, red and golden yellow, we'd dress in heavy wool sweaters and puffy parkas, don mittens and caps and gather around the blue spruce in the front yard. We'd smile as my father snapped photo after photo, pictures to be used for the home-made Christmas card my mother sent out each year. After my father finished developing them in his dark room in the basement, my mother would pick the best one and send it out to our family and friends.

But behind that carefully crafted image was another story. We hated taking the annual Christmas card photo. For one thing, it took hours. My mother arranged and rearranged our position around the tree as my father took dozens upon dozens of photos. The fall air was thick and we sweat under our winter clothing. As we shifted our bodies around the tree and tugged at our itchy wool sweaters, my mother criticized the way we smiled. She chided us for closing our eyes at exactly the wrong moment. Afraid to speak up, we swallowed our anger only to have it leak out when one or another of us began to cry. And yet, year after year, their friends commented on what a wonderful photo it was.

It took a long time for me to have the courage to see what I did not see back then. What I could not allow myself to see. Behind the representational circles and squares of the genogram, behind the façade of a middle class life was the struggle to be seen, to make a connection that all the money in the world could not buy. Although my genogram lay out the structure, the real work was just beginning.

A year after my mother's death, I sat in the living room of my friend's house, tears streaming down my face. I felt knotted up inside, threads of grief, shame, guilt and sadness twisted around my heart. I was overwhelmed by her loss and I did not understand why, even after she was gone, I still clung to feelings about her that no longer served me. I wanted to understand why I'd struggled so with my mother. Why the hollow ache in my heart would not go away. Why I wanted her acceptance so desperately and why I felt so powerless to do anything about it. And so I began to write.

Although I have traveled this road with hundreds of families, it was not until I chose to do it myself that I could learn the lessons I needed to learn. As I peeled back the layers of my own life, I began to see things I had not seen before. I was forced to confront family myths that I'd always held to be true. I discovered that what I'd believed to be the whole truth of my family story was only partially true; that there were things I chose not to remember. Stories that had been readily accepted. Patterns of behavior that were destructive and challenged the image of the idyllic family life I remembered. Until I began this journey, I could not see the role I'd played or the way the decisions I made so long ago still impacted me.

Now I share those stories with my students. My classroom is filled with people from all walks of life, people who come from families who are every bit as diverse and unique as the other. As I tell them stories about my own life, I encourage them to share stories of theirs. To ask questions, to be curious, to learn to speak their truth. Stories, I tell them, have the capacity to connect us, to bridge the divides we feel and allow us to understand. As my students share their stories, they begin to accept one another and as many times as I watch it happen, it always feels like magic. Because no matter how different we appear on the outside, inside we are all human.

Years ago, when I held that genogram on my lap, I believed that I had avoided the suffering that my classmates had experienced. That the heartache and pain they felt had not touched me, but that was not true. None of us escape hardship because all of us are human and there is pain in humanity. My journey was one I could not have predicted. The struggle to understand my own distress gave me the opportunity to accept my family for who they are, not who I wanted them to be. And now, rather than clinging to the knots of grief, anger and sadness, I am left with a compassion for the people they are and an acceptance and appreciation for the experiences we had together.

It has been two years since my mother's death. As I write this, on the eve of Mother's Day, it is as if a weight has finally been lifted off, one I have been carrying for as long as I can remember. I feel a lightness I have never felt before. Writing this book changed me. Claiming one's story will do that. I believe it can change you too. And so I invite you, the reader, to come along while I share my story. It is my hope that in sharing my journey you will have the courage to begin your own.

# Chapter 1

## *The End and the Beginning*

I was not ready to be an *orphan*.

A few years ago, when my friend Judy's father died, she'd used that word too. At the time I thought it was ridiculous. She was almost 60. Surely she didn't need her parents anymore. But now, as I faced a life without mine, I understood what she meant. It was hardly unexpected. Nineteen years had passed since we'd seen the first signs of Alzheimer's disease. I'd had nineteen years to get ready and yet…

I closed my eyes and took a deep breath, allowing the warm air to pass through my nostrils, trying to prepare myself for what was to come. As I exhaled and stepped inside my mother's dimly lit bedroom, I felt frightened. The room inside the nursing home was claustrophobic, the air acrid and stale. This small, shared bedroom was a far cry from the airy, light-filled one she'd slept in with my father. I remembered looking out their bedroom window into the dense landscape of trees that surrounded the house on Rockledge Road in northern New Jersey. The birch trees dancing in the summer breeze. The birds stopping to eat at the large redwood feeders my father hung from the eaves. It had always seemed so peaceful to me. And although we had tried to warm up the sterile space she slept in now, it never felt like home. I shook myself out of my memories and turned my attention to my mother who lay in the bed, her mouth agape; the sound of each breath like a wave smashing against the shore. I took off my coat and draped it over the wheelchair tucked away in the corner, the chair she needed to use after she broke her hip and could not relearn to walk. She wouldn't be needing it anymore.

I pulled up a chair and sat down next to the bed. Above her head there was a photo taped to the wall. My mother and father in happier times, her deep brown eyes twinkling with joy as she smiled at him. This woman, the one who lay in my mother's bed, barely resembled the mother I knew. Her face contorted. Her eyes vacant. She sounded like a freight train chugging up a mountain.

The phone rang at 9:00 that morning. I'd been up early, drinking coffee and looking out at the snow that blanketed my brother Robert's small and peaceful back yard. "You're mother's condition has taken a turn for the worse," the nurse said, her voice measured. "I've just left her. We have her on oxygen to help with her breathing. We've given her some morphine to keep her comfortable."

I hung up the phone, closed my eyes and felt my ribs expand as I forced a deep breath. I had been anticipating this call for weeks and yet, somehow I still felt unprepared. "Rob?" I said into the air. "Rob?" My voice sounded small and childlike. I walked up the two flights of stairs to my brother's bedroom and called again, pushing my voice out into the cavernous space at the top of the stairwell. "Rob?" We gathered our things and drove in silence along the tree-lined Delaware

River. The branches were barren, the sky a dull grey. "This is the end," I thought to myself. This was surely the end.

A month before, as I sat in a noisy English pub in San Francisco, my cell phone rang. It was December 23rd. My husband Bob and I had taken our sons into the city for our annual Christmas celebration. It was a tradition I'd continued from my own childhood, when I lived near New York and we spent each Christmas Eve in the city. We'd been to the theatre and to look at the decorations in Union Square. When my phone rang, I excused myself from the table and found a quiet corner where I could talk undisturbed. I pressed the phone against my ear. It was the doctor. My mother had been in the hospital for a week or so, dehydrated and running a high fever. The doctor had been in to check on her and wanted permission to run some tests.

"She has an advanced directive," I said, but he didn't seemed to be listening. It wasn't the first time I'd had this conversation. While I railed at the medical staff from 3,000 miles away, my brother and sister took turns sitting beside her.

I hung up the phone and called my brother Michael who lived in Boston. "I just got off the phone with the doctor," I said. "I don't know how much longer Mom's going to be..." My voice trailed off. "I think you need to visit her," I said, hoping my words would encourage him to go. It had been years since he'd seen her. 'It's not Mom,' he'd said when I'd asked him why it had been so long. 'She isn't there anymore.'

I knew what he meant. It had been years since she'd shown any signs of the mother who had raised us, but as his older sister I couldn't bear the thought that he might never see her again. Over the years I'd worked with so many families who were haunted by cutoffs from the very people they loved. I wanted to protect my brother from a lifetime of regret.

Michael drove down the next week and spent a few hours sitting by her side. I'd booked my tickets for a trip back to New Jersey to see her in mid January, but now I wondered if I should go sooner. Could I get back in time to say goodbye? Each day when I called to check in, my sister and brother expressed concern that the medical staff was ignoring my directive. I'd spoken to countless doctors and nurses. "I am her medical surrogate," I yelled, "You do not have the right to do any of this without my permission." But it seemed like one hand did not know what the other was doing. Every day felt like Groundhog Day, each day the same as the one before. As Christmas turned into New Years, I slept with the phone next to my bed, waiting for the call that did not come. Eventually after what seemed like dozens of phone calls, I got her released from the hospital. Hospice was called. Now it was just a matter of time.

But by mid-January she was still hanging on. On January 13th, I sat beside her in the day room of the assisted living facility. She was unusually sleepy, dozing off through much of our visit. I spoke to her gently, stroking her hand and thinking back to the days when, as a child, I lay with my head in her lap feeling her manicured nails on my scalp as she stroked my hair.

"Her breathing is labored today," I said to the nurse as she passed by us.

She paused for a moment to listen. "Bea," she said, trying to rouse her, but my mother continued to sleep. "I'll keep an eye on it," she promised.

"I'll see you tomorrow, Mom," I said after an hour or so. I gave her a kiss on the forehead and said goodbye. I'd be back again tomorrow.

The next day Robert and I arrived around ten o'clock. My mother's eyes were closed. She appeared to be sleeping.

We pulled a couple of chairs beside the bed and sat down. Someone had slipped a CD into the player next to the bed. An aria from Puccini's La Bohéme played softly. The oxygen machine hummed in the background. I turned up the volume to drown out the sound. A few minutes later my sister Elisa arrived.

"We're all here, Mom." Robert said, but she did not respond.

The nurse came in and updated us on what we already knew. *Overnight things got worse. Her breathing became heavy. Labored. They were trying to slow it down so she didn't have to work so hard. They'd given her morphine to make her comfortable. One dose, but so far it wasn't helping. Another one was scheduled for 11:00.* The nurse promised she would call the doctor to see if she could give her more.

Despite the flurry of activity around us, in that moment, time appeared to stand still. People came and went. Robert, who was in the middle of final preparations for a performance of a musical he had written, left reluctantly to go to rehearsal. "I'll be back as soon as I can," he said. A hospice nurse sang to her and stroked her head. A priest came in to give her last rights. As he stood at the head of the bed and made the sign of the cross, he anointed her with holy oil on her hands, chest and forehead. *"Through this holy unction may the Lord pardon thee whatever sins or faults thou hast committed."*

"Our father, who art in heaven, hallowed be thy name," my sister and I prayed. I'd memorized the words of the Our Father as a small child. They rolled off my tongue without meaning, a mantra that didn't work anymore. I found myself floating, as if I was watching the whole thing from high above. As if I wasn't really there. When the priest left, I returned to the side of the bed and reached out to touch her arm. The skin on the back of her hands was slick from the holy oil. I rubbed it in, gently.

A nurse unwrapped the stethoscope from around her neck and reached down to check my mother's heart rate. A caregiver, a young African American woman with long dreadlocks pulled back into a ponytail leaned over my mother and kissed her on the forehead. "Oh, Miss Bea," she said softly, tears streaming down her face. A young man brought in a bucket of drinks and a plate piled high with small cubes of yellow and white cheese, crackers and pepperoni. They would remain untouched.

"Let us know if there is anything we can do for you," he said.

What could anyone do? The room smelled of death. The steady hum of the oxygen machine. My mother's breath. My sister, who worked as a massage therapist, rubbed her feet. "They're turning blue," she said and pulled the cover over them again.

Things turn blue. Feet. Hands. I did not know this. As the body shuts down it focuses its energies on the most important areas, the lungs and the heart, pulling all the resources where it is needed the most. I focused on my mother's rapid and labored breathing, trying to will it to slow down. "Dad is here," my sister said. "I can feel him. He's here to take her home." I hoped that she was right.

How long would this go on? How long *could* this go on? Outside of this room life continued. The sun poured through the large cheery windows of the dining room. The residents gathered for lunch. They sat at square tables with bright yellow tablecloths and ate turkey and mashed potatoes and steamed green beans. Less than a month ago, my mother would have been out there too.

She'd forgotten how to chew. For months she was fed a pureed diet, small piles of unrecognizable mush, like the food you feed a baby. "Open up Mom," I said, resisting the temptation to make airplane sounds when I lifted the spoon to her lips. But in the past month she had stopped eating altogether. They called it 'pocketing her food'. I imagined her shoving brussels sprouts into a napkin, the way we did when we were younger, waiting to feed them to the dog when no one was watching.

My phone buzzed, startling me and pulling me back to the present moment. It was my friend Andre. *"The San Francisco 49ers have just hired Chip Kelly to be their head coach,"* he texted. Andre and I were always talking about sports. It occurred to me that he did not know where I was. No one knew. As if things were normal, I messaged him back. *"Chip Kelly? That's a mistake."* The phone buzzed with his reply and again I responded. The messages continued to come. Buzz, buzz, buzz. Again and again I responded until I could no longer pretend.

I reached over and turned up the music a little louder. Puccini's aria took me back to Sunday afternoons when we were young, my mother's opera playing on my father's old hi-fi stereo and a warm fire crackling in the fireplace. My sister and I held hands. She reached for my mother's foot through the covers and I placed my hand on her shoulder.

"It's OK," we said to my mother again. "We'll be OK. It's time for you to rest."

I wondered if she could hear us. I closed my eyes and breathed in unison with the oxygen machine. In and out, as though somehow my breathing with her, for her, could make things just a little bit easier. In and out. In and out. A chill ran through my body and I noticed, for the first time all morning, my mother's breathing had slowed down.

My sister said that angels surrounded her in her moment of transition. "Dad and her parents were there to greet her," she said when it was all over. Elisa seemed so certain, but I was not so sure. I felt batted around the way one does when caught in the undertow. Trying to steady myself, I focused on her breathing, listening as it slowed. In and out, in and out. And then it stopped.

"Mommy," I cried. "Mommy." It felt like my heart was breaking.

Elisa and I sat for a while in silence. We held hands and wept openly. Waves of memories crashed over me and although we were there together, in that moment I felt alone, like a small child abandoned on a doorstep. My parents were gone. I wondered who would take care of me now.

After a while I stepped outside of the darkened room into the blinding light of the hallway and reached into my pocket for my cellphone. I had to let the family know. I rubbed my eyes and searched for the number for Uncle Vic, my mother's brother. "Mom is gone," I said when he answered the phone.

My mother was gone.

The next few days were filled with phone calls and meetings and funeral arrangements, visiting with family and sharing stories about my mother. After the funeral we gathered together in a small French café in New Hope, Pennsylvania, just across the river from my youngest brother Robert's home and toasted my mother's life.

I looked around the room at the faces gathered. I thought about the roles she had played in our lives. A sister, a friend, a colleague. An aunt and godmother too. My mother's brother began to speak. "She was my star," he said, his voice breaking. Soon his own tears forced him to stop. My brother Robert read one of my mother's newspaper columns that she had written many years before. It was an essay about Jonathon Livingston Seagull, the book by Richard Bach that shares the lessons Jonathon learns about life and flight.

I read a piece I had written for her a few years before, when she was already in the nursing home and could no longer recognize me. "*I wanted to send my mother flowers for Mother's Day.*" I began, "*The house we grew up in was surrounded by flowers; big beds of brightly colored zinnias, snapdragons that stretched to the sky and delicate, orb shaped peonies...*" The words caught in my throat. Although we were all grieving, I felt alone in my sadness. I couldn't help feeling that no one could understand what I was going through.

And then, as if sensing my aloneness, my sister asked those gathered to fold their napkins in half and place them on their heads. She was reminding us of a part of my mother that I loved, an anomalous part that I had wished she showed more often.

"Place the points over your forehead," she said, demonstrating. "Welcome to The Cardinal Club."

One night, when my father was away on business, my mother picked up her cloth napkin, folded it in half and draped it over the top of her head with the point facing downwards, towards her nose. "Put your napkins on your heads, kids," she said and of course we did what we were told. I glanced around the table, looking at my siblings as they looked at her. "It's time for a Cardinal Club meeting."

"A what?" we asked.

"A meeting of the Cardinal Club. You are all now members."

And that was that. We'd all been inducted into her private club. From that point on, when my father was away from home, we would wait patiently for her to call a meeting to order. Right in the middle of dinner, between forkfuls of pasta and sips of milk, when we'd be recounting tales from band practice or the day's cross-country meet, she'd place her napkin on her head and the energy would change. We always looked forward to Cardinal Club meetings although none of us can remember why. My mother had never been silly, but the memory of her sitting there, the worn point of the cloth napkin trailing down towards her nose, still makes me smile.

Back in the restaurant, we tapped our spoons against the sides of our wine glasses. "The meeting will now come to order," my siblings and I said in unison.

After the funeral I flew back to California and placed a photograph of my mother on the sideboard, beneath my collection of Italian Deruta pottery, a passion I shared with her. It was a picture of her on Sanibel Island in Florida, her hand cupped around a collection of tiny shells she'd just gathered on the beach. I lit a candle and said a silent prayer and then went about picking up where I'd left off, straightening up the kitchen, throwing in a load of laundry and getting ready to teach the next day's classes. Now I had the added responsibility of settling her estate. There were decisions to make, papers to file, documents to sign and dozens upon dozens of phone calls. I stayed busy.

But back at home in California, things took on a surreal quality. Far removed from the chain of events I had just been through, life had continued. It was as if someone had pushed pause for a few days and now it was time to start again. January turned into March. I flew back to New Jersey to clean out the storage unit where we'd condensed what remained of my parents' lives.

Ten months after my mother's death, I had lunch with my friend Bill. It was a warm day in October and we sat at a small table in the back of a riverside café. Bill and I had known each other for many years, since we'd worked together as family therapists in the late 1980s. He was soft spoken, tender and kind, different from most of the men I knew. He'd always been so easy to talk to. In the old days we'd spend hours sharing our clinical work and even more time talking about our lives. But in recent years we hadn't spent much time together and I hadn't seen him since my mother passed away. So much had happened.

"I'm sorry about your mom," he said.

"I was with her, you know, when she died. I've never been through that before. It's really…" I couldn't think of the right word.

Bill smiled. I'd always loved his smile. His face had changed over the years. His blonde hair was now grey. The eyes that had captivated me all those years ago had sunken slightly. He complained about the pain in his knee. He was having surgery soon, he said. Life has its way with all of us.

"It's not the way it looks in the movies." I continued. "It's not… peaceful." Or at least it didn't feel that way to me. My mother's death had been loud and caustic. For months after she died, I couldn't get the sound of her labored breathing out of my head, the heavy pounding and groaning, pounding and groaning as she labored on. Even in her death, my mother filled up the space around her. I felt the words catch in my throat and my eyes fill with tears. Even though it had been almost a year, it still felt so fresh.

"My relationship with my mother was so complicated." I said. "When my father died it was different. I had just had the most amazing visit with him. We talked about so many things. I felt, for the first time, that I really knew him, knew who he was. But with my mother… I'm not sure I ever knew her. I'm not sure she ever knew me."

I picked at my Salade Niçoise. "I kept myself so closed off from her." I continued. She always felt like a Death Eater, like someone who could suck out my soul. "I never let her get too close because being with her always felt so dangerous."

In the months after her death, I'd been trying to write about her, as if putting her down on paper would keep her from disappearing. She had been sick for so long, her personality stripped by the dementia. I was worried that my children wouldn't remember her. I was worried that *I* wouldn't remember her, as if her dementia might spread and erase everything that had come before. But the words weren't coming. I started essay after essay but nothing was working. I felt confused and overwhelmed. I kept losing my way.

"Why can't I ...," I said to Bill, but he cut me off before I could finish.

"It's too soon," he said.

"Too soon?" I said. "What are you talking about? She died in January. It's October, for god sakes. It's the only thing I've *been* thinking about for months."

"I'm not talking about thinking," he said. "You have to forgive her. You have to forgive yourself."

Bill's words hit me right between the eyes. I did not want to admit it, but there it was, right in front of me. The simple truth that I hadn't allowed myself to see.

"When my father-in-law died," Bill said, "I remember walking outside onto the porch of his house. We were close. He was a friend to me. I remember thinking, this is all wrong. Everything is all wrong."

I looked away from my friend as he spoke. I could feel the tears welling up in my eyes. This too was all wrong.

"This is grief," my wise friend said. "This is what grief looks like."

In the months after my mother died I'd felt numb, not at all the way I'd felt after my father's death. His had rocked me to the core. I felt lost, like I was floating away, unable to ground myself in time and space. My body ached from the hole that his death left in all of our lives. But my mother's death had been different. I'd spent months settling her estate, sorting through paperwork, paying bills and talking to attorneys. There had been the storage unit to unload. Her belongings to distribute. There were so many things to do I couldn't see what should have been obvious, what, as a therapist I had helped so many of my clients do. I couldn't see that I had not allowed myself to grieve.

My mother was 79 years old when she died. Although she was in her early 60's when we noticed the first signs of dementia, it was in the nine years after my father's death that things truly began to fall apart. Nine long years of watching her disappear into this most horrible disease. You might be wondering why I hadn't prepared for that moment. Why still, after all those months, I hadn't let myself grieve. More than two years later, I'm just beginning to understand.

As I watched her slip away, I went through the motions. I helped make plans for her care. I navigated the legal and medical challenges as best I could. I visited her faithfully. Although I never got comfortable seeing her, I held her hand. I sang her songs. I kissed her on the cheek. I tried to do what any good daughter would do. I tried to do what was right.

But each time I saw her, I slipped back into the defensive posture I had maintained throughout my life. The dynamic I hated with all my heart. Even in her dementia, my response was automatic. I was angry at her for getting sick. Angry at my father for leaving us to deal with her. I was angry that my mother would not give me the kind of relationship I wanted to have with her and then, when it was too late, I was angry that she no longer could.

The truth is, as strange as it sounds, I don't think I ever stopped hoping that things would change. That she would see me as an individual filled with ideas and dreams and things I was passionate about. I never stopped wanting to share those things with her, to show her the woman I had become.

As a child, when I did something she disapproved of my mother would say, "I love you, but I don't have to like you." It's taken me a long time to understand what those words meant, how they've stayed with me, locked away deep inside. I knew my mother loved me. Of that I have no doubt. But I wasn't so sure about the second part of that sentence. It wasn't until after she died that I realized I'd never stopped hoping that one day she would like me too.

I guess it should be no surprise that I dedicated the next 30 years of my life to practicing family therapy. I began my career working with children who struggled with drugs and alcohol, depression, anxiety and fear, but I soon realized that my ability to make change was limited if I did not include their families and so I studied the masters; Salvatore Minuchin, Jay Haley, Carl Whitaker and James Framo. As I continued to work with children, I began to ask their families to come in. Mothers and fathers. Grandparents. Aunts and uncles. Whoever I needed to create change, to heal the family system. And to my surprise, they came.

In those years I witnessed stories of anguish and joy. Frustration and tremendous growth. The pain of the stillbirth that lingered fifteen years later. The shame of a secret never shared. The grief of a family who lost their daughter to AIDS. A promise made to a dying mother that could not be kept. These were the experiences that cause pain and limit our capacity to connect with one another.

Over those years I sat with hundreds of families and helped them to reframe their stories to allow for the possibility of healing to occur. I marveled at their courage, at their willingness to go to difficult places, to dig deep into a collective memory and say things they had been afraid to say. To listen to things that are difficult to hear. To sit in the silence of not knowing what comes next. It was not easy and I never lost sight of the gift it was to be able to witness those moments of grace. But as skilled as I was in helping other families, I could not do it with my own family. I was too afraid.

It wasn't for lack of desire. I'd rehearsed it many times. I imagined bringing my entire family together, my mother and father, my brothers and sister. We'd sit together and hash through the hard stuff. We'd say the things we hadn't said. We'd talk through the scars of childhood. They were there. Sure, there'd been plenty of good times. Wonderful times in fact, but there were scars. Everyone has scars. And as we talked to our parents, as *I* talked to *my* parents, they would listen. Really listen and understand. And things would get better between us. I would let down the wall I'd built, the thick brick wall that I felt every time I looked into my mother's eyes. And she would see me, really see me, for who I am and not the person she wanted me to be. That's all I ever really wanted.

There'd been a moment with my father, a connection that helped me find closure, but it never happened with my mother. There were times that I tried. Times when I stuck my toe in the water to see what would happen but it had blown up in my face. My mother could not hear me. There was no room for my truth in our family. And so I gave up. And as much as I wished and dreamed and hoped, I remained silent. And then it was too late.

For almost twenty years my siblings and I watched her disappear as Alzheimer's erased every part of her. It started slowly. A missed word here. A forgotten moment there. Soon it was names and faces. Entire conversations and then, the sound of her voice. But although it should not have come as a surprise, I was not ready for it to be over. There was still so much work to be done. So many things left unsaid. I was always waiting for the right time. It was never the right time.

My mother died on January 14, 2016. After she died I found myself swimming in a sea of grief, unsure how I would move forward and wondering what my life would be like without her. I was 56 years old and still clinging to the hope that one day we would have the connection I'd always dreamed of.

A year later, left with a relationship I wanted to understand and a lifetime of stories to work with, I did the only thing I could think to do, I began to write. I do not think I am alone. I know from my experience as a social worker and family therapist that every family has their own story. That these stories are rich in joy and pain, in exhilaration and heartbreak. That they contain experiences that both connect and divide us and I have come to know that it is in sharing these stories, in having those sometimes hard conversations, that we can build the bridge back to one another.

I began my journey with one story. I ended with another. I have tried to do what I had hoped to do so many times, to say what I had been unable to say. I have tried to speak my truth in the hope that I would find my mother in my own story and myself in hers.

These are the conversations we never had.

# Chapter 2

# *First Signs*

The family room of my parent's home on Sanibel Island was littered with clothes and books and piles of crumpled wrapping paper. Dylan, my youngest, sat near the artificial Christmas tree, an open box from Lord and Taylor, my mother's favorite department store, on his lap. His thick blond hair and swimsuit were still damp from an afternoon of swimming in the Gulf of Mexico.

"Thank you Nana," he said, gazing up at her. At eight years old he had a cherub's face and big brown eyes that sparkled when he smiled.

For many years now we'd come to my parents home on Sanibel Island to spend the week between Christmas and New Years on the gulf coast of Florida. As two of my siblings and I had kids of our own, we'd celebrate the Christmas holiday at our own homes and then fly to Florida for a family vacation. With the four of us living in different places, it was the only time each year when our families were all together.

Sanibel was my mother's sanctuary. My parents bought the island home when they were nearing retirement, looking to find a warm place to get away from the cold, snowy winters of New Jersey. Unlike what most people think of when they think of Florida, Sanibel was different. There are no giant amusement parks or all you can eat buffets. Accessed by a long causeway from Fort Myers, Sanibel is a relatively peaceful island, 11 miles long and filled with bike paths, golf courses and sandy beaches with some of the best shelling in the world. My mother, who never wanted to be included in the group of blue haired snow birds who escaped the winters of the northeast to places like Orlando, Miami or Fort Lauderdale, chose this place precisely *because* it was different. Sanibel, as she often insisted, was *not* Florida.

As I sat on the floor and watched Dylan carefully unwrap the packages my mother had given him, I grew more and more concerned with each one. Inside this box was a girl's grey cardigan sweater with a wide neck and small pearl buttons. In fact, each box he opened contained clothing for a little girl, certainly not appropriate for her 8 year-old grandson.

As he reached into the box and pulled out the sweater, I could feel my brow furrow while I looked on in disbelief. Was I really seeing what I thought I was seeing? I scanned the room to see if anyone else had noticed and found my brother Robert looking in my direction. I locked eyes with him, praying he could read my mind. I tried to maintain a neutral face, but I had never been very good at that. 'You should never play poker,' a friend once told me and of course, I knew when he meant. I grabbed the sweater from Dylan's outstretched hand and quickly tucked it back in the box, but it was too late. She was watching us.

"Try it on," my mother coaxed, smiling. She crossed her arms and leaned back in her chair, clearly proud of herself. She wore a smug expression that had always annoyed me. Dylan took the sweater from the box and obediently began to pull the tiny sleeve over his suntanned arm. My mother waited, watching as he stretched it awkwardly over his body. Clearly it didn't fit. He looked at me, sheepishly.

"Stand up," she directed and of course he did what he was told. "Do you like it?"

"Yes, Nana," he said. The name "Grandma," was far too common for my mother. She'd chosen the name "Nana" when she became a grandmother.

Suddenly the room got eerily quiet. A moment before there had been laughter and conversation as everyone unwrapped their own presents, but now all eyes were on Dylan. For a moment the silence was deafening. He stood beside me, his lean body seeming to tax the seams of the sweater. He didn't flinch. He didn't laugh. He didn't say a word. He just stood there as if nothing was wrong at all.

I was overwhelmed by his love and understanding in that moment. Dylan adored his Nana. Both my kids did. Although it would still be years before we would acknowledge what was happening to my mother, Dylan knew it was not about him. He did not want my mother to feel embarrassed or ashamed. While my relationship with her was anything but easy, the kids were a great buffer between us. She wasn't your typical grandmother. She hadn't spent hours babysitting or hosting sleepovers so that my husband and I could get away for a weekend. She didn't make cupcakes or take the kids to the park or to see the latest Disney movie. She did with them the things she liked to do herself. She taught them to hit a golf ball and to drive the golf cart. She talked to them about baseball. She read them books and she bought them clothes.

My brother Michael caught my eye. I turned towards my father but he was watching her. I closed my eyes for a moment and prayed no one would say anything out loud. I didn't want Dylan to be embarrassed. My sister Elisa mouthed something to Robert under her breath. Michael just shook his head. It felt like the air was slowly being sucked out of the room.

"You can take it off," I said to Dylan when my mother stepped away to start dinner. I helped him pull off the sweater and shoved it back into the box. I prayed he hadn't realized what was going on.

"Dad," I said, when she was out of earshot, but he didn't let me finish.

"She just got confused," he interrupted. "She must have been in the wrong department, that's all."

It was a mistake. An error. A momentary slip. But the soft grey sweater with the sweet pearl buttons could hardly pass for a young boy's clothes. Something was terribly wrong. And although we all must have been thinking the same thing, no one dared to challenge my father. I was still afraid of him. Perhaps the others were too. We'd been raised to honor and respect and yes, even fear our parents. To challenge him would be unacceptable. The rules had always been clear. We knew our place. And so we remained silent.

My mother loved Christmas. When we were kids, she hung huge pinecone wreaths and gold papier-mâché angels over the fireplace, decorations that she and my father made by hand. There were stockings on the mantel and a big Douglas fir in the corner of the living room. Every Christmas she made dozens of cookies: spritz and snowcaps, gingerbread men and jelly tots. We decorated the gingerbread with frosting and hung them from the tree and every year she hosted a big party for all their friends complete with Christmas caroling. On Christmas Eve we'd go into New York City to see the Nutcracker ballet and out to dinner at an Italian restaurant. We walked up 5th Avenue to watch the ice skaters at Rockefeller Center and see the big Christmas tree, stopping at St. Patrick's Cathedral to kneel and say a prayer by the manger. We'd attend midnight mass and every Christmas morning we'd awaken to piles of presents under the tree, one for each us, wrapped in our own special paper.

The tradition of gathering together for the holidays extended long into adulthood. After they bought the house in Sanibel, my parents began to celebrate the holidays there. It wasn't the same, of course. We were still expected to come home, families in tow, but despite the colorful decorations on the island and the artificial tree my mother decked with shell ornaments and candles, to me at least, it never really felt like Christmas.

Although my mother bought all the presents and wrapped every one, she never asked us what we wanted for Christmas. Like she did with everything else, she made those decisions herself. In truth, I was never sure my father even knew what was in all those boxes. Now, as an adult, I wondered why. Had he not been interested or had she just not trusted him? There were always plenty of presents. If there were 6 presents for me, there were the same number for Michael, Elisa and Robert. No one would feel shortchanged. Now, with the 3 spouses and 6 grandchildren, the list had gotten quite a bit longer. She started shopping in the summer, buying things on sale and tucking presents away until she had a half dozen or so for each of us. She bought clothes, for the most part. There might be a book or two, a set of espresso cups or a piece of jewelry, but clothing was my mother's specialty.

At the risk of sounding ungrateful, I never liked the clothes she gave me. My mother had lousy taste in her own clothing, a penchant she enthusiastically imposed upon her daughters. Elisa and I would often get the same things in different colors. One year she gave us sweaters. Mine was black with horizontal purple and blue stripes, a sweater that was guaranteed to make me look 10 pounds heavier. It was also two sizes too small.

"Do you like it?" my mother asked.

"Yes." I lied. I was smart enough to know that *yes* was the only safe answer.

Detecting the hesitation in my voice she asked, "What's the matter with it?"

"It's not really my style," I said, trying to be gentle.

"Oh yes it is. It will look great on you."

"Well, actually, I think it's a little too small." I tried another approach.

"You just need to lose a little weight," she quipped.

Of course we weren't really talking about the clothes. She didn't care about my taste. She didn't want to know what I liked. My mother's presents were a reflection of her, of how *she* saw *me*. How she wanted me to be. How she felt about me as her daughter. And my response was, in her eyes, a referendum on how I felt about her. If I didn't like what she gave me, it meant I didn't like *her*.

We never returned anything. She would never have allowed it. For better or for worse, that black sweater with the blue and purple stripes was mine, whether I liked it or not. And so, year after year, that sweater, like most of the presents she gave me, sat in my closet with the tags still on it, waiting for one of two things. Either I would lose enough weight to fit into it or I would muster up enough courage to donate it. Not surprisingly, neither ever happened.

Now I wondered what I had been afraid of. I lived 3,000 miles away. There was almost no chance of her ever finding out. It is only recently that I have come to understand that I'd bought into that system. I did not challenge the status quo. I could not risk the consequences. Instead, the clothes hung in my closet, sometimes for years. Some of them still do.

But this year's gift giving disaster was an entirely different matter.

We had dinner that night, the way we always did when we were there, on the big screened-in lanai at the back of the house that overlooked the swimming pool and the sixth hole of the Beachview golf course. My father's orchids hung from the branches of the ficus trees, the pale yellow and purple blooms splayed across the green background like one of Monet's landscapes. We passed around roast beef, salad and baked potatoes. We drank glass after glass of red wine and chatted about the day's activities, but none of us dared mention what had just happened. Instead, it hung in the air, like a dark storm cloud about to break open.

I couldn't wait for dinner to end. I wanted desperately to talk to my siblings about what had just happened but in secret, the way we had so often as children. Tucked away in our bedrooms at the top of the stairs, we'd whispered our anger at our parents, words we could never say out loud. And so, after dinner, while the grandchildren watched a movie and my parents cleaned up the kitchen, their adult children gathered around the dinner table with a fresh bottle of wine from my father's collection. And although all of us, including our spouses, had seen what had happened, it was my siblings and my conversation to have.

She was our mother and the boundary around our nuclear family system had always been rigid. Over the years the spouses joked about their role in our family. "We're like Muggles," my sister-in-law quipped a number of years before, referencing the term from the Harry Potter books. "No matter how long we're around, we'll never be magical." It was true. Despite years of being part of the family, they still felt on the outside. What was happening with our mother was our problem to deal with; Michael's, Elisa's, Robert's and mine.

"It's getting worse," I reported. "A few weeks ago, when I was on the phone with them, she completely forgot what we'd just talked about."

My parents always called on Sunday. Most days the call started with the both of them. We'd say hello, catch up and then without fail, my father would hang up, leaving my mother on the phone to hear what was going on.

"Mom will fill me in later," he'd say. "I'm going to say goodbye now. Talk to you next week."

But in the last few months I'd noticed that he'd been staying on the line a lot longer, oftentimes for the whole call.

The Sunday conversations were carefully scripted. My mother would start with asking how I was. "Fine," I'd say, or "busy," or "OK," anything so as to not provoke more questions. I'd give her a 'Reader's Digest version' of what was going on with me, a brief overview that didn't encourage discussion. "You know," I'd say. "Working a lot, that sort of thing." She didn't know my friends. She didn't really understand what I did for a living and I didn't want to take the time to explain. She had opinions about everything. Over the years I'd learned that if I gave her even the tiniest opening, I'd find myself in defense mode, fighting back unwanted advice or what felt like judgments about anything and everything I was doing. It seemed like nothing I ever did was good enough.

Instead, I'd talk about the kids. "Tucker had a baseball game on Friday," I said, offering my oldest son's activities to change the subject. "He went 1 for 3, with a double."

My mother loved baseball. She'd grown up a Brooklyn Dodger fan, living just a pitcher's throw from Ebbet's Field. She often said that when the Dodgers moved to Los Angeles it broke her heart. When the Mets became New York's National League team, she transferred her allegiance to them. That was the team she raised us to root for. In a sea filled with dangerous topics, baseball was one of the few things I felt safe talking to her about.

"And Dylan? What's he up to?"

"He's great." I said, my voice uninspired. "He's playing baseball too, left field. He's got a great arm. The other day he threw somebody out at home all the way from left field."

We talked for about 20 minutes. I went through the motions, covering the checklist of things we usually discussed. School. The weather. Any field trips the kids had been on. Report cards would be coming out soon.

"What about you?" I asked, when I'd run out of things to say.

After my parent's retired they'd started splitting their time between their home in New Jersey and the house on Sanibel Island. They played golf, went to the beach, had a subscription to the local symphony and regularly entertained their friends. They were Eucharistic ministers at their church and were both presidents of their respective leagues at the Beachview Golf Club. For retired folks, they always seemed to have a lot going on.

"So how are the boys?" my mother asked a few minutes later.

"Bea," my father snapped. "She just told you."

"Oh, of course," she'd said. There was a moment of awkward silence, a window, perhaps, to express concern about her memory lapse, but I kept quiet. There was no room to discuss things like that. Seconds later the moment was gone. My mother changed the subject and we continued on as if nothing had happened.

Christmas vacations on Sanibel had a familiar flow to them. We rode bicycles and went to the beach, hunted for seashells and went out to dinner, but as normal as this one seemed on the surface, the concerns about my mother's memory kept popping up, setting off alarms throughout the week. Earlier that afternoon, before we opened the Christmas presents, I came back from the beach to find her huddled by the refrigerator with Dylan, repeating a story that she'd told him over breakfast just a few hours before.

"Did you know your Nana used to be a writer?"

"Of course he knows that, Mom," I said. I was irritated and impatient.

"Why does Nana repeat herself so much?" Dylan asked when we were alone.

"She's just got a lot on her mind," I said. I wanted desperately to believe it was true.

As we sat around the table that evening, I told my siblings a story my father had shared during a visit a few months earlier about a time, earlier that summer, when my mother had gone to the grocery store to pick up a few things for dinner. She was gone for a long time and my father was frantic. He called everyone he could think of, wondering where she could be. When she returned home a few hours later and without any groceries, she couldn't tell him where she'd been.

"And then there was the time that she bought Tony and me matching women's bathrobes," my brother Robert added. "They barely came down to our knees. They had great big, monogramed letters on them, but they weren't even our initials." At the time it seemed funny. "We put them on and paraded around the room. Everybody had a good laugh." But now it didn't seem so funny anymore.

The more we talked, the more worried we grew. Still, we knew enough to know we couldn't confront her. To say she was guarded would be an understatement. When we were kids, she used to sing "Put on a Happy Face," a song from the musical *Bye Bye Birdie*. She was careful about the face she presented to the outside world. She was proud and confident and she wanted the world to see her that way too. She didn't believe in showing vulnerability. She never admitted her mistakes. In fact, in all the years I'd known her, I don't think she ever said she was sorry.

My father staunchly defended her. His role had been to provide for us and, as was common practice in the 1960s and 70's, he'd left the raising of the children to her. He was her backup. We approached him cautiously. He was serious and stern, not the kind of father who read us stories or played ball with us in the yard. While my mother handled most of the discipline, she'd include him only when necessary and we lived in fear of that.

But ever since he'd retired, he'd really softened. He had been short tempered and quick to anger, but now he smiled more often and there were less flashes of the anger I remembered. The change in him was lovely for me and for the first time in my life I began having conversations with him. We shared a love of cooking and he knew a lot about wine. He began to build model ships in his workshop in the basement and he loved to tease his grandsons.

But despite the softening boundaries between us, there remained a formality to our relationship. A line I didn't cross. We had been raised to respect our parents and that's what we did. I was still careful about what I said to him and how much I shared. We had different political views, different ways of seeing the world, but when I disagreed with him, I rarely said so. The few times I'd tried had backfired. It would take something extraordinary for me to risk upsetting the status quo. It didn't matter how old I was or that I had children of my own, I never forgot he was my father.

As our time on Sanibel Island wore on, there were other incidents that concerned us. By the end of the week, there was still no plan in place for what to do next. I wasn't at all comfortable with that. Somebody had to say something. As the oldest, it was up to me. I chose the timing carefully. I looked for a chance to talk to my father when he was alone. The day before I was to leave, I found him in the garage smoking a cigar and working on the hull of one of his ship models.

"Dad," I said, my voice hesitant. "We're really worried about Mom. We think she should go to see a doctor."

"She just went for a checkup," he said. He furrowed his brow and raised one eyebrow, the way he did when he wanted to make a point. I think he was hoping to reassure me, to convince me he had it under control.

"And did she talk to him about her memory?"

"She said she did," he answered. "And the doctor said she's fine. She just has a lot on her mind."

It was the same line I had used to explain my mother's behavior to Dylan just a few days before. I looked at my father suspiciously, but I didn't continue. He didn't want to talk about it and like a good daughter, I knew enough not to press.

And that was how it all started. At the time my mother was in her early 60s, young, by any stretch of the imagination. She had just retired and was about to begin the second chapter of her life. In the next few years they would travel to Egypt and host friends for dinner, comb the beach for coquina shells and play golf. They planned on a wonderful retirement.

But what might have been a chapter filled with many pages of adventures was not to be. Two years after my father's death a doctor confirmed what by then we already knew to be true. Scrawled across his report was the diagnosis "Alzheimer's-like dementia," a disease that would one day rob her of the very essence of who she was.

# Chapter 3

# *The Gospel According to Bea*

I tugged on the heavy oak doors of the Church of the Immaculate Conception. Once inside I found a spot against the back wall and waited for the rest of my family to come inside.

*"A reading from the holy gospel according to Matthew."* The priest's voice boomed through the church loudspeakers. There was a rustle of papers, a shuffle of bodies and the thud of a kneeler or two as the congregation rose to its feet and the priest began to read. I pressed my body against the back wall of the church and waited. We were late.

We were often late for church. Maggio time was not the same as normal time. We were late for school and doctors' appointments. We were late for dinner reservations, Girl Scout meetings and field trips. The truth was, we were late for almost everything. We were late so much that it became normal "They'll wait," my mother used to say if we complained, as if nothing ever happened until we arrived. Lateness was in our DNA.

When the priest finished reading, the congregation took their seats, settling in to listen to the homily. The church was full, but now that people were sitting down, I could see a few empty spots here and there towards the back of the church where we were standing. But there were six of us. My mother looked around, fixing her eyes on a pew at the front of the church, a spot in the second row, just to the left of the altar. She motioned to my father.

"Mom," I whispered. "Can't we just sit there?" I pointed to a partially empty row just a few feet from us. Maybe she hadn't seen it. "Mom," I said again, trying to get her attention. "Please." I was begging now. But as usual, my mother had other plans. She smiled forcefully, her teeth clenched, her jaw tight; the smile that meant only one thing. We were going to do things her way.

Why did she always have to choose a spot in the front of the church? I shook my head softly and rolled my eyes. The older I got, the more her behavior bothered me. Now that I was in high school, it mortified me. I argued with her silently. Why couldn't we just slip in unnoticed? Pretend we were there all along? Why couldn't we just blend in the way other people did? But I already knew the answer.

My mother always wanted to be the center of attention. The soloist in the choir. The lead in the school play. She was Mimi in La Bohéme. "We called her Queen Bea," my uncle once told me. "She was a star." She had been that way since they were kids. My mother did *not* blend in.

As soon as everyone was seated, my mother began her procession down the aisle. For a moment I held back, wishing I had the courage to stay put. I looked over at Michael as if together we might initiate a small coup, but who was I kidding? I dropped my head and took cover, allowing my long brown hair to sweep across my face and then I fell in line. My mother strode down the aisle like an actress sweeping across the stage, her head held high. She always liked a big entrance. When she arrived at the second row, she paused and waited while a young family slid down to make room.

I prayed the ground would open and swallow me whole. I protested silently, saying the things I would never say aloud. *This was ridiculous. If mass was so important, why couldn't we ever be on time? And if we were late, because we always were, did it really matter where we sat? Couldn't we get the same thing out of it if we sat in the back?*

But the truth was, as much as I hated to admit it, that wasn't the point. My mother wanted people to see us. Coming in late didn't bother her. She had always been great with the ad lib. She knew how to capture the moment. As she strode down the aisle, her family in tow, the spotlight was all on her. She *wanted* people to notice. She *needed* people to notice.

We were garden-variety Catholics, which is to say, we were hardly devout. Like many kids I knew, I'd gone to Catechism on Saturday. I memorized the ten commandments and learned to say the rosary. I'd even been confirmed. We went to mass each week and said grace each night at dinnertime. *Bless us o' Lord, and these Thy gifts which we are about to receive from Thy bounty.* We mouthed the words in a unified monotone as fast as we could. Dinner was waiting.

I'd spent my elementary and middle school years in Branchburg, a fairly close-knit, rural community. Back then, Branchburg was a quaint township, with rolling hills and family farms and it was decidedly white. But Branchburg didn't have its own high school. Instead, the students were bussed to the nearby town of Somerville. Unlike rural Branchburg, Somerville was the city, with businesses and shopping centers, apartment buildings and government offices.

As far as I could remember, there'd never been any discussion about where I'd go to high school, at least none that

I'd participated in. After 9 years of public school, my parents sent me to the nearby Catholic school, Immaculata. Unlike the parents who sent their kids to Catholic school from a sense of deep spiritual commitment or religious faith, my parents simply believed that I'd get a better education at a smaller, Catholic school, and they had been right. I'd done things at Immaculata I would never have done at the larger school. I'd joined clubs, acted in plays and had even been the drum major of the marching band. With just 700 students, the smaller pool had indeed been an easier one for me to swim in.

But at the same time, there had been something else in play, something they dared not admit, at least not out loud. Despite the fact that they'd grown up in Brooklyn, or perhaps because they did, they were uncomfortable with the public school. It had a much more diverse student body, a blend of race and socioeconomic status very different from the community I grew up in. Although they never said so out loud, I think the unpredictability scared them. They'd worked hard to craft a childhood experience of opportunity filled with all the things they valued and they were not about to leave anything to chance. My parents respected excellence and exceptionality. They appreciated travel, culture and the arts. They valued structure and routine. A clear hierarchy and well-defined roles.

That evening as we sat down to dinner, the phone rang. "Maggio residence, Suzanne speaking," I said, the way we'd been instructed to.

The word "residence" still made me smile. It sounded sophisticated and a tad snobby. It conjured up a gated property, with rolling lawns and a tennis court, a swimming pool and an old stone guest house. We lived in a two-story white stucco on Preston Drive, in a neighborhood of working class families. It was an older house built in the 1920s and updated here and there through my father's less than perfect handiwork. Despite a lack of carpentry experience, there was nothing he wouldn't tackle. He built wall-to-wall bookshelves in the dining room and stained them in a dark mahogany brown. He finished the basement with a patchwork of blue and green stick-on carpet squares. He tiled the kitchen floor in handmade tiles that my parents brought back from a trip to Italy. But the bookshelves were slightly crooked. The carpet squares came unglued and the tile floor cracked periodically because my father, who'd never lay tile before, installed them over the original, uneven Formica. My siblings and I slept in bedrooms that were built in the converted attic space complete with slanted ceilings, a bathroom shower that leaked and a salvaged air conditioner that froze solid if you ran it overnight. It wasn't perfect, but it was home.

Cell phones and computers did not exist yet. My mother served dinner each night at 6:00, shortly after my father came home from work. We ate our meals around a large, round, butcher-block table. In the summer months she cooked tomatoes, zucchini and Swiss chard that my father grew in the garden at the back of our acre property. My mother, who was a really good cook, used food as an expression of love. Her meals were plentiful and abundant and designed to make you overeat. She expected us to clean our plates, to have seconds and sometimes thirds. To eat until the food was gone. On the rare occasion when we'd pass on seconds, she'd say, "What's the matter, don't you like it?" It was code. What it really meant was, *don't you love me?*

Dinnertime was sacred, a time for our family to be together and talk. I had friends whose families ate in front of the TV, setting their plates on little fold out trays, spread out on their laps or on the coffee table. But that never happened at our house. In the evening, when my father came home from work, he would change his clothes and head to the liquor cabinet to mix a couple of perfect Rob Roys. They shared a cocktail every night and a glass of wine or two with dinner. Their cocktail hour was sacred, a time for them to sit and talk and we knew enough to leave them alone. Like a loyal chief of staff, it was during this time that my mother updated him on our day. By the time we got to the dinner table he was briefed and ready to go, a general reviewing his troops.

"I understand you got your science test back?" he said.

The week before, we'd spent a tearful few hours in preparation for the test, reviewing what happened when you combined certain elements on the periodic table. Both my parents had gone to college. While my mother helped us with English and writing, my father was a chemist, science and math were his responsibility. My father was smart and methodical, but he could also be impatient. The top executive at a large chemical company, he spent his whole day solving problems. By the time he got home, he had little patience left for us. His tutoring sessions always started out fine, but they often ended with me in tears, frustrated and angry. No matter how hard I tried, science never came easy.

"Yes," I answered. "I got a '92."

"Only a 92?" he asked. He raised one eyebrow. "What happened to the other 8 points?"

He wasn't kidding. He was a difficult man to please. I was, by most measures, a well-behaved child. I never did any of the things my classmates did. I didn't drink or smoke. I never cut school. I hardly ever even talked back. A conscientious student, I worked hard . There was an occasional C, but for the most part, I earned As and Bs. When report cards came home it was my father who signed them, sometimes including a note to my teacher.

They weren't much for praise. A few years ago I found my old report cards, tucked away in a tired manila envelope at the bottom of a drawer. My mother had given them to me many years before. I pulled one out the other day and slid the thick blue card from its well-worn sleeve. While there were several notes from my teacher, "Very dependable, good attitude" and "It was a pleasure to have you in my class," there was only one note from my father. At the bottom of a report card with more 2's than 1's, the grades given in that year, was a note to my fourth grade teacher, Mr. Oakley. "We've spoken to Suzy about her efforts," he wrote. "She has promised that she will do better." Perhaps that is why I carried around the constant sense that I was never quite good enough.

Years later, when I had kids of my own, I told them those stories. We laughed when they handed me their report cards. "You know what grandpa used to say to me," I reminded them. The boys did well in school, but the truth was, I pushed them hard too. Like my father, I'd always wanted them to be better. Now I wondered if I they also felt like they were never good enough.

I'd jumped up when the telephone rang, eager to end the conversation about my science test. "May I speak with Dr. Maggio?" the voice on the other end said.

"Who may I say is calling?"

"Dad," I said, remembering to put my hand over the receiver, "It's Mr. Firing."

"Tell him I'll call him back," my father said sharply. He didn't like to be bothered when we were eating.

Phone calls at dinner were common, especially for people trying to reach my father. Other than his close friends, most people referred to him as "Doctor" Maggio, the title he had earned when he received his PhD in Organic Chemistry from

Yale. Having a chemist father was kind of fun. Over the years he'd come to my class to do science experiments. My favorite was a volcanic explosion of foam that he made by mixing two clear liquids together. Don't ask me what they were.

By the time I was seven years old he began a career in public service as a Somerset County Freeholder. In New Jersey, freeholders are responsible for county governance. It was supposed to be a part time job, but it soon became our identity. My parents pledged their allegiance and ours, to politics and the Republican party. The man on the phone, Mr. Firing, was one of five freeholders who served with my father on the board and he called the house often, but it was also just as likely that my father would get calls from a host of other important people. There was Mr. Ewing, our assemblyman and Mr. Bateman, our state senator. County department heads would call and when they did, we were my father's support staff. We answered the phone and carefully took messages and sometimes, when he didn't want to be bothered, we even ran interference. "He's not home right now," I lied. "May I take a message?" It was all part of the job.

I hardly remember what life was like before my father entered politics. The night he won his first election, my mother piled us into the tan and brown Country Squire station wagon and we drove to the Somerville Inn to watch the returns. Election night was a school night and although the polls didn't close until 8:00 p.m., we wouldn't have missed it for the world. Even my grandparents would be there.

My father, who was coming from a full day at work, met us in the parking lot of the Somerville Inn. He pulled open the heavy double doors and we stepped inside. My mother helped us off with our coats and handed them to the lady at the coat check right inside the door. She'd dressed us that night, as she often did, in matching clothes she'd made herself. Elisa and I wore long sleeve dresses with white patent leather shoes. Robert and Michael looked sharp in their Nehru jackets. It was 1966.

The main ballroom was noisy and packed with people I didn't know. It was all a little overwhelming. I spotted my Grandma Basili, standing by the entrance to the ballroom. She smiled and waved, making her way across the room to where we were standing. My mother's mother was petite, only about 5 feet tall. Unlike her daughter she was soft spoken and preferred to be out of the limelight. She wore a wig to cover up her thinning hair and a hearing aid that beeped when she hugged you. She was gentle and kind and I loved it when she tickled the inside of my arm while I tried to keep from laughing.

My mother's father was from Rome. He was handsome, of medium height with a lean build and pencil thin mustache. He came to this country as a young man and had never returned. He loved sports, especially baseball and once worked as a sports writer in his native Italy. He wore dark rimmed glasses and spoke broken English with a heavy accent. When we weren't watching baseball together, he'd spend hours in the yard bouncing a soccer ball on his head. He'd kick it over the roof and then send me, over and over again, to retrieve it.

My father's parents were a little less colorful. My grandfather Maggio was a New York City postman and Grandma worked as a secretary for an insurance company. Like my mother's mother, they were second generation Sicilian. Both families lived in Brooklyn, my mother's on Maple Street and my father's on the Queens border in Ridgewood. My father's parents still lived in the brownstone on 68th Avenue but by then my mother's parents had moved to Yonkers, north of the City. The first in his family to go to college, he had been a dedicated student. My grandmother used to tell me that she had to tell him to shut off his light at night and go to sleep because he stayed up so late studying. They were extraordinarily proud of him and they wouldn't have missed this moment for anything in the world.

We followed closely behind as my mother and father walked through the crowd and made their way to the front of the ballroom. My father was leading as the early polls began to come in. A large black chalkboard filled the front of the ballroom with a grid filled with numbers and the names of the precincts in the county; places like Bedminister, Bernardsville, Peapack and Raritan. On the left side of the board were written the names of the candidates, both state and local.

My mother pointed to my father's name written in block letters at the top of the chalkboard. "This is where they keep track of the votes," she instructed. I grabbed my brother Robert's hand and followed my mother as she led us behind the board, to a space that backed up against the wall of the ballroom. It was a frenzied scene, with a dozen or more people answering telephones, jotting down numbers on slips of paper like bookies at the racetrack and sending them by runner to the main room. "These people are receiving the counts from the precincts," she explained. "As the votes come in they add them to the board."

People milled about, chatting and sipping cocktails. My mother guided us to a table near the front of the room and left us with our grandparents. She joined my father and they began to work the room, shaking hands and making small talk. My father was on the quiet side, but my mother made up for that. She was articulate and confident and she could carry on a conversation with anyone. Throughout the campaign she had worked just as hard as he had. They really were a team.

A cheer rang out each time a new precinct reported. In this sea of adults, we were the only children and everyone wanted to meet us. "You must be Suzanne," people said, as they came by to say hello. "It's a pleasure to meet you." I might have been only 7 years old, but I felt like a celebrity.

Every now and then we'd wander around, squeezing between the tall bodies to check out the board or get something to eat. We found a bowl of rainbow mints in the hallway and filled our pockets. We played hide and seek behind the couches and overstuffed chairs in the foyer. By ten o'clock, it was clear that my father was going to win. There was a lot of cheering and toasting with champagne, but by then we were thoroughly exhausted. Robert, who was almost three, fell asleep on my grandmother's lap. Finally, when the rest of us could barely keep our eyes open, my grandparents took us home.

Two months later, on a snowy New Year's Day in 1968, my father was sworn-in in the main courtroom of the Somerset County courthouse. As sunlight streamed through the large windows, there was an almost spiritual quality to the proceedings. We sat in the front row, clothed in the matching outfits my mother had sewn for the occasion. Judge Rizzo entered the room, dressed in flowing robes. With a bang of the gavel, the meeting was called to order and my father took the oath of office for the first time.

The next day, the local paper ran a picture on the front page. It still hangs over my writing desk, all these years later. My brothers are dressed in plaid, my sister Elisa and I in matching white dresses. We were all so young. My thick brown hair is bobbed short and barely touches my neck. We are clustered around my father, our eyes fixed on him. Elisa and Robert, who were around 3 and 4 at the time, stand on a chair. Elisa holds the Bible. I have many photos of us taken over the years.

Photos of me in my Girl Scout uniform, leading the Pledge of Allegiance. Photos where I am taller and older and my hair much longer, but of all of them, this one is my favorite.

This is when it all began. The day we were baptized into the faith, a religion carefully crafted by my parents. Unwittingly, we pledged allegiance to the things they held dear. We did not question. There was no room for dissension, no space to share an alternate view. There would be no *I*; there was only *we*. My parents demanded loyalty at all costs. To their ideals and a specific set of rules. Of course I did not notice it at the time. It was only after many years of studying family therapy that I began to understand what was true about my family. We were a closed system, a rigid hierarchy with a boundary so tight that no one could get in. Escape was nearly impossible. It would be many years before I would understand just how those moments would shape my sense of self. How they would teach me lessons about loyalty and belonging that I would struggle with for the rest of my life.

I was 9 years old the first time I remember having to defend my father's politics. He had been in public service for more than a year by then. Richard Nixon was running for president and I showed up for school with a box of red, white and blue "Nixon/Agnew" buttons for everyone. I marched into Mr. Oakley's fourth grade classroom, my head held high, and took my seat right in front of my best friend, Martha.

"You're voting for Nixon?" she sneered, her voice dripping with disapproval. "You've got to be kidding."

"Of course," I said confidently.

As a child, my parents' values were my gospel. I never questioned their beliefs. I never challenged their perspective. In politics as in life, they were always right. I was a Republican as sure as I was a Maggio. There was no other way to be.

"Martha says she's voting for Humphrey," I announced when I came home from school that day. I had spent the better part of the school day arguing with her. I was angry that she wouldn't listen. I wasn't sure how we could stay friends.

"Martha's family is Democrat," my mother said, the disapproval apparent in her tone. She might as well have said Martha's family were martians. Democrats were *other*. Democrats were *different*. Democrats didn't know any better. They just weren't as smart as the rest of us. And although I didn't really understand what she meant, I accepted her assessment without question. Of course, she was right. Unlike most of my friend's parents, Martha's mother was divorced. Unlike my mother, Martha's mother worked. She never went on field trips or brought cupcakes to school. They lived in a small house in town and although we stayed friends through high school, I didn't remember ever going to visit. Martha's family *was* different. If only Martha's mother knew what my parents knew. Surely then she would understand what I understood. What we all knew to be true. It would take many years for me to understand that in my mother's world, *different* really meant *wrong*.

Six years later Nixon resigned amidst almost certain impeachment. I had campaigned vigorously for his reelection, manning the phone banks at Republican headquarters and canvassing neighborhoods on weekends. But by then I was a sophomore in high school and Nixon's resignation blended into a montage of theatre rehearsals, band competitions and Advanced Biology exams. It wasn't until many years later that I learned of my father's profound disappointment with the man he had once staunchly defended.

It took a few more years and an acceptance to Boston College for me to begin to understand just how narrow my worldview had been. For the first time I was surrounded by people who were truly different from me. In those late night conversations in my dorm room I began to understand that not everyone saw things the way my parents had. That a person's values had a lot to do with their life experiences, the way they had grown up and the things they had been exposed to. While I had grown up sheltered from many of life's difficult moments, my friend Martha's life had been quite the opposite.

Back then, the world was black and white. In politics and in life, there were two sides to every battle, my parents' side and the wrong side. I stood by them blindly, never thinking to question their perspective. I pledged allegiance to their political views. My father was honest and direct and people trusted him. That he always won reelection by a large margin was evidence of that. We were immensely proud of him. When he introduced legislation that would bring a new vocational school to the community, the paper ran an editorial praising his efforts. When New Jersey Governor William Cahill wanted someone to head a commission for a brand new state lottery, the first in the nation, it was my father he chose. There had even been talk of a run for governor.

In high school I worked as a page in the library. I spent summers working in the snack bar at the county park and filing in the personnel office. As the daughter of a politician, getting a job was easy. There was no application. I just had to show up. I was Dr. Maggio's daughter, after all. We received complementary tickets to New York Mets games and invitations to the symphony. On snowy days, when the roads were impassable, a snowplow showed up to plow our driveway. When we needed a plumber early on Sunday morning to pump out our backed up septic system, we didn't have to wait. One call and the plumber was on his way. We were part of a very select group and membership had its privileges.

But it also came with responsibility. Our parents reminded us that everything we did reflected on them. Because my father was a public figure, people were always paying attention. We were not Suzanne or Michael, Elisa or Robert, we were Dr. Maggio's children. "We are the first family of Somerset County," she once said to me.

I learned to carry on polite conversations with people I barely knew. I campaigned not just for my father, but for the entire Republican ticket. I spent hours manning the Republican booth at the 4-H fair, shaking hands and handing out bumper stickers. In high school, after an afternoon of band practice or play rehearsal, I worked the phone bank at campaign headquarters. "Hello Mrs. Wilson," I said, reading from the script. "My name is Suzanne and I'm calling from Republican headquarters. Can we count on your vote this November?"

Sometimes I persuaded a friend to join me. What was normal to me was novel to them and having a friend along made the hours go by quickly. There was an undeniable electricity to campaign season and it was easy to get swept up in it. But the truth was, participating had never been a choice. I did what I was expected to do.

Carved wooden elephants, the symbol of the Republican party, stood on the bookshelves. Campaign paraphernalia filled our closets. The walls of my father's office were covered with photographs, a shrine of celebrities he had met throughout his political career. They attended presidential inaugurations and galas at the State House. There were signed photographs of Governor Cahill and President Ronald Reagan and former A list entertainers from my parents' generation, Ann Margaret and Jack Benny.

We lived according to their gospel. Like Moses and the 10 commandments, the rules couldn't have been clearer. They demanded loyalty above all else, to them <u>and</u> to the family. I did what they asked of me. I believed what they told me to believe. I valued what they wanted me to value. We had a good life. They gave us opportunities that many of my friends could only dream of. My parents were confident and self-assured and their certitude made me feel safe and protected. I followed them blindly until the day when I couldn't do it anymore.

# Chapter 4

## *Tug of War*

I could tell something was wrong the moment I closed the door behind me.

"Sit down." My mother's voice was terse. "Your father and I would like to talk to you."

It was the winter of my sophomore year at Boston College. I was home for Christmas and just back from spending the afternoon shopping with my boyfriend. My parents sat at the kitchen table. The air was thick with anticipation. They had been waiting for me.

"What the hell is the matter with you?" my father snapped. His anger frightened me. "We raised you to be better than this."

"What is this about?" I asked. I sounded like a six year old.

"We know what you have been doing with Chris." My mother's voice shook as she spoke.

Chris and I had been dating for a year. He was handsome, with blonde hair, big brown eyes and a toothy grin. He had a dimple in his cheek when he smiled and I was crazy about him. He was a year older than me, a baseball player at his university who I'd met during the previous summer when we'd worked together. I'd been surprised when he'd asked me out and I fell for him almost immediately. It was the longest relationship I had ever been in and by far the most serious. We'd spent a lot of time together that first summer and once we both went back to college, we'd managed to make the relationship work long distance. Most of the time I traveled to see him, catching a ride with a friend who went home almost every weekend to see her boyfriend in New York City so I could spend weekends with Chris.

I'd been a fickle teenager when it came to dating. While most of my friends seemed content to "go steady" with one person or another, my relationships never lasted more than a month or two before I would lose interest. In fact, there'd been so many of them that years later, when I met my husband, he'd taken to referring to my former boyfriends by number just to keep track of them all. Despite all the boys I'd been involved with, I was still a virgin the summer I met Chris.

I hardly knew anything about sex. As a Catholic, I had been taught that sex was to be saved for marriage and sex outside of marriage was a sin. My mother had never lived on her own. She went straight from her parents home to marrying my father. There'd been no "birds and bees" conversation in our house, no mother daughter chat where sex was concerned. Perhaps she was as uncomfortable with the subject as I. What little I did know, I'd learned in school when our middle school gym teacher taped a piece of paper over the small window in the classroom door and, to the horror of all the girls in the room, held up a sanitary napkin and explained that soon we all would be entering something called puberty.

I was unprepared for adult intimacy. In college, prompted by one of my roommates, I bought a copy of the classic book

*Our Bodies Ourselves*, written by the Boston Women's Cooperative. I blushed as I flipped through the pages. It all felt slightly daring and dangerous. Although it was uncomfortable, I couldn't look away.

In the fall semester of my sophomore year, I travelled back and forth from Boston to Manhattan to visit Chris almost every other weekend and although we slept in the same bed during those visits, I'd always made it clear that I wasn't ready for sex. As old-fashioned as it seemed, I believed what I had been taught and Chris, for the most part, seemed to understand. But as my feeling for him grew deeper, I began to question the limits I had set for myself. Was it really such a bad thing? This wasn't a casual relationship. I loved him and he said he loved me too.

Of all my friends in college, I was, by far, the most conservative. I kept myself in check. I steered clear of wild parties. I went to nearly all of my classes and I stayed away from things that could get me into trouble. It had worked so far, but when it came time to figure out what to do in my relationship, my inexperience was glaring. I asked my roommates for advice. "Should I, you know?" I said one evening as we sat around the dorm room on the second floor of Gonzaga Hall. I couldn't even say the words. "Have you…" I blushed with embarrassment. They just laughed.

"Do you love him?" they asked, although I wasn't entirely sure that it mattered to them.

"Yes," I said. At least I thought I did.

"Then what's the big deal?"

I was 20 years old, living on my own and in a long-term relationship with someone I, albeit naively, thought I might marry. To have sex at this stage of my life, my friends suggested, was normal. But the truth was, to me it wasn't that simple. It was more than just church doctrine. I had been raised to do the right thing, to follow the rules, to act responsibly, even if I didn't always want to. I cared deeply what others thought of me, what my parents thought of me. For most of my childhood, the rules seemed clear. Somehow, this was different.

We talked about it again and again. After what seemed like weeks of conversation, I finally convinced myself I was ready. One afternoon I took the Green Line into Boston and walked, for the first time, into Planned Parenthood. As I sat on the edge of the examining table, my eyes wandered around the room nervously while I waited for the doctor to come back with my first prescription of birth control pills. I tucked them in my backpack and rode the trolley back to campus. By the time I returned home in December, Chris and I had had sex just a couple of times.

"I love him," I said, trying to sound strong and confident, but my voice was shaky and uncertain. At that moment there was no adult me, that had vanished the minute I walked into the room. Seated in the chair across from them was the child I had always been, would always be, in their eyes. It did not occur to me to ask why they thought they could pry into my business. Why they felt they could treat me in that way. Instead I allowed myself to be cross-examined, chastised for a crime I had not committed.

"Love?" My father's voice dripped with disgust. "What do you know about love?" He stood up from his chair. His imposing body towered over me. His chest heaved with emotion. "He's using you. You're no better than a whore, giving yourself away like that. Have you no respect? For us? For what we taught you?"

My mother sat at the table, her face turned toward me, her silence saying more than words could ever say. She was just 21, barely a year older than me when she'd left home to marry my father, a young woman who'd never gone away to college. They'd reminded me many times how they'd given me opportunities they'd never had. Did they not understand that those freedoms and experiences had shaped me and helped me grow into the person that sat in front of them? Somehow none of that mattered now.

"You are a slut," my father continued, his eyes steeled toward me. "He doesn't love you. He's just getting what he wants from you. He'll use you up and spit you out."

I sat in stunned silence. His words sliced through me with a pain that reverberated through every cell in my body. I was ashamed and embarrassed. I wanted to jump out of my skin, to disappear into the floor. As his words swirled around me, I felt paralyzed. I wanted desperately to escape but I could not bring myself to leave. At first I tried to argue, to tell them Chris wasn't like that, that they had misjudged him and me, but they would have nothing of it. I had disappointed them. Rejected what they had taught me.

I waited until they finished and then stood up and walked silently out of the room, my legs buckling beneath me. I was sobbing now. Tears ran down my face and soaked the top of my t-shirt. Devastated by my father's words and my mother's silence I was filled with self-contempt. But with each step I took, the rage inside me grew. I hated them in that moment. Hated everything they stood for. I was tired of being their daughter, of shouldering the enormous responsibility of living up to their expectations. They didn't even know me. I walked up the stairs to my bedroom and closed the door behind me.

"What's wrong?" my sister asked.

I told her what had happened. "They said you told them. That you found my birth control pills and asked Mom what they were." I struggled to get the words out, my body heaving through the tears. It had been part of their assault on me. *I was supposed to be setting an example for my brothers and sister. They looked up to me. What, my mother had asked, was she supposed to tell them?*

"I did not," Elisa said, but I didn't believe her.

I went back to college still feeling shaken and somewhat disoriented. I was afraid to tell Chris what had happened. Afraid he would stop coming by. The last weeks of the Christmas break had been awkward, but I'd gotten through it. Now, back in Boston, I vacillated between outrage and self-hatred. I spent hours talking to my roommates who were stunned by my parents' behavior. They were critical of them and protective of me.

"You have the right to make your own decisions," they'd said. "You haven't done anything wrong."

But as hurt as I was, it was difficult to shake my parents' condemnation. The truth was, I was an extraordinarily compliant child. My high school years had been marked with good grades and squeaky-clean activities. I was in the Drama Club and the Spanish Honor Society. Even though I was miles away in college and living on my own, I felt beholden to them, to their trust in me. I carried them with me. It was as if I could feel them on my shoulder, watching my every move. I faithfully attended my classes. I studied hard. I tried hard to be a good daughter. I'd done everything they'd asked me to do. I wanted to make them proud.

But now, for the first time, I found myself at a crossroads. I'd followed my heart and made a choice that my parents could not understand. It was as if I'd ventured outside the safe zone and immediately stepped on a landmine. I hadn't acted irresponsibly. Quite the opposite, in fact. I'd thought long and hard about what I wanted. I'd been conscientious and careful and it still had blown up in my face. My relationship with my parents was in tatters. My confidence shattered. My heart ached.

A month after I returned to college, I received a letter from home. I recognized the handwriting as soon as I pulled the envelope out of the campus mailbox. It was from my father. We hadn't spoken much after that night, keeping our conversations to a minimum throughout the remaining weeks of the winter break. Back at college, I tried to return to the life I had created far away from home. Although I was still angry at the way they had treated me, I was besieged by the guilt I felt for destroying their trust in me and as much as I tried to let it go, I couldn't. It hid in the corners of my room. It popped up as I lay alone in the darkness and though I continued my relationship with Chris, it infected every phone call and visit.

I walked a few steps down the long corridor of the student union and tore open the envelope. It was a Peanuts card with a cheerful picture of Woodstock on the cover, a 'Just stopping by to say hello' message on the inside. "Dear Suzanne," my father wrote, his familiar calligraphy rising from the page. "I'm sorry for what I said," His words were concise and to the point. "I love you very much, Dad." Heat rose in my cheeks. My hands began to shake. I stood alone in the hallway of the student center and I cried.

I've always wondered if my mother knew he had sent it. Had she encouraged him to? And if so, why hadn't she signed it? My mother's extended silence spoke volumes. Her tacit agreement, clear. But I too had been silent. I had not stood up for myself. I did not engage in my own defense. At the time I did not think I had a choice. I was expected to shove my feelings aside and get back in line, the way we were always expected to. Still, as hurt as I was, his apology was something I would never forget. I didn't know it at the time, but something had begun to shift in me, the beginnings of a crack deep under the surface. It wasn't until many years later, as a young social worker, that I began to understand what was happening. I had begun to individuate.

My father never brought it up again. I finished the semester in Boston and came home for the summer vacation. The following year I would be leaving to spend a semester in England. I would be studying English literature in the country of Shakespeare and Chaucer. My parents, who had taken us to Europe three times by then, were thrilled.

It wasn't until I was in England that I felt, for the first time, truly on my own. I wandered through the streets of Exeter, stopping in the market to pick up a wedge of traditional cheddar or loaf of freshly baked bread. I sat in the kitchen with my British classmates and discussed Jimmy Carter's botched attempt to rescue the hostages in Iran over pots of freshly steeped Earl Grey tea. When I wasn't reading D.H. Lawrence or attending a seminar on Shakespeare, I spent the better part of those six months traveling by train to as many places as my Eurail pass would take me. I hiked the fjords of Norway in the snow and ate pretzels in a square in Salzburg where scenes from the Sound of Music had been filmed. I wandered through the Louvre and the Uffizi and ate pizza on the streets of Rome with my Italian cousins Elisabetta and Paola and a handful of their friends. In the middle of the semester, my parents came to visit. I showed them the English countryside and we caught up over spoonfuls of clotted cream, strawberry jam and freshly made scones of a traditional Devonshire Cream Tea. I loved every moment of it.

After a semester abroad, reentry was difficult. I suppose it was inevitable. I'd spent months on my own, surrounded by a culture I had only imagined. If going away to college peeled back the covers to expose a freedom I knew little about, my semester in England tore them off completely. I danced late into the night with my British classmates, sipped glassfuls of sherry and downed pints of lager and lime over conversations that exposed me to ideas I had never even considered. It was as if it took an ocean to allow me the distance I needed to see things more clearly. With each month I gathered more confidence. I tried things that scared me. I took risks I could never have imagined. And through it all, I developed a courage I had not known before. No longer surrounded by my tribe, I began to see myself as separate. Now, back in the fold, I felt myself shrinking again. It was as if I had grown too large for the space I was allowed to occupy. For a while I tried to hold on to the me I found in England, but over time I melded back into the familiar shape I had held for so long.

Already an English major, a study my mother had also pursued, I decided to add Art History to my schedule. In the fall of my senior year, I applied to the MFA program at the University of Chicago and to my surprise, I was accepted. My parents were ecstatic. It was everything they had wanted for me. But it was not to be.

As I embarked on the spring semester of my senior year, something else began to call to me. A Jesuit University, Boston College had a strong social justice focus, a commitment to the service of others. Some of the people I knew were planning a trip to Appalachia to do a week of volunteer work with the Glenmary Missionaries in the mountains of Kentucky and Georgia. That spring, instead of returning home to spend Easter break with my family, I climbed into a van with a couple dozen fellow students and made the 10-hour drive to Clarksville, a small community in rural Georgia. I do not remember if I asked my parents' permission to miss the holiday with my family. I do not know that it would have mattered. I only knew that I had to go.

The poverty we were exposed to was staggering, unlike anything I had ever seen before. As a child I had driven past the slums of New York, seen the tenements from a distance, but this was different. These people had nothing. They lived in houses with dirt floors, with windows covered in plastic. There was no running water. They heated their houses with wood and many of the homes had outhouses instead of bathrooms.

The shock of these images shook me to my core. How could I have not known about this? I had seen pictures of poverty in other parts of the world. Children with distended stomachs. Houses made of cardboard. But that happened in other places, not here in our own country. It was something I would never forget.

We spent the week insulating houses as best we could, covering windows with double layers of plastic sheeting and chopping wood. We brought food to the elderly and visited with shut-ins, listening to stories about their families and often meeting their children and grandchildren. In the evenings, as we gathered in the local church basement, we reflected on what we had seen. Although these people had nothing, I was struck by their kindness and generosity. Almost instantly, I felt a kinship with them.

"Folks is folks," one of the men said one afternoon as we chopped wood together. His words became our mantra for the week. There was a simplicity here, a kind of rawness and truth that stayed with me long after the week had ended. As we worked side by side, we talked about our families. We laughed together and even shed a few tears. Despite being from different socio-economic worlds, we really were just the same.

By the time I got back to Boston, something inside me had shifted. I'd felt alive in Appalachia in a way I never had before. I found meaning in the service work and I wanted more of it. As the days and weeks went by, I realized I could no longer do what I had intended to do. Graduate school would have to wait.

After I returned from Appalachia, I applied to the Peace Corps and the Jesuit Volunteer Corps Northwest. I wanted to do something to make a difference in the world. It sounded cliché, but the spark that ignited on that trip to Georgia was growing stronger. By now I'd started volunteering at an inner city after school program in East Boston and spending my free time with the group I'd gone on the trip with. I even began to understand my faith differently. I'd always felt detached from the Catholicism I'd grown up with, but now I began to understand it in terms of social justice, a cornerstone of my Jesuit education. I had even started going to mass again, something I hadn't done in all the time I'd been in college.

One afternoon, as I stood in the kitchen of my apartment on Commonwealth Avenue, I worked up the courage to call my parents. "I have to talk to you guys about something," I said, my voice shaking. "I don't think I'm going to go to graduate school, at least not right now." I tried to soften the blow. They had been so excited when I'd told them I wanted to study Art History. I knew they would be disappointed.

I paced the kitchen floor as I pressed the phone to my ear. I chose my words carefully. I would be going to Montana to work in a children's home, I told them. It would be for a year. The organization would provide me with room and board and a small stipend in return for my service. I wanted to do something to make a difference in the world. It was what I felt called to do. After I finished, I waited for their response.

There was nothing but silence.

"Are you there?" I said after what seemed like an eternity.

"What the hell are you talking about?" my father said breaking the silence. His voice sharp and disapproving and dripping with judgment. "Why would you throw your life away?"

"I'm not," I said. I sounded like I was six years old again, sucked back into the family vortex I could never seem to escape. My heart was racing. "I want to…"

"We didn't raise you for this," my mother chimed in.

"This is not what we spent our whole goddamn lives working for… so that you can go off and… How are you going to take care of yourself?" my father continued.

My father's words felt like arrows shot into my heart. I knew they would be disappointed, but I never expected this. I couldn't think of anything to say. I listened as they berated me. When they finished, I hung up the phone. I'm not sure I even said goodbye. I stood paralyzed in the silence of the small kitchen, my body heaving with tears. Their condemnation rang in my ears. After everything they had done for me I had let them down again. It was as if I was suspended between two universes, wanting desperately to belong to both. I loved my family. My connection to them filled every cell in my body. Like the very oxygen I breathed, I did not believe I could survive without them, but at the same time I could not deny the voice inside that was calling to me. I had to follow.

My roommate Missy came in. She was listening in the next room.

"It's your life," she said, after I finished telling her what had happened. "You have the right to decide what you want to do with your own life." She reached out and gave me a hug.

After graduation I stayed in Boston and got a job waiting tables at a local restaurant. I didn't want to go back home.

Perhaps I didn't trust myself. I had been unable to hold my ground when it came to my parents. The pull of my family system was too strong. I couldn't risk what might have happened if I allowed myself to get sucked back in. Later that summer, I packed my bags and drove cross-cross country with a friend. Through the long miles of highway, through Ohio and Indiana, Wisconsin and Minnesota, my eyes were fixed firmly on the road ahead.

I have often joked that I ran away from home when I was 21, putting as much distance between the East coast and myself as I could. It was all I could do to catapult myself from the suffocating grip of a family that I loved desperately but could not separate from. It was a matter of survival, a zero sum choice. Loyalty meant everything to my parents, but loyalty to them meant I could not be true to myself.

What I didn't realize at the time but understand now is that you cannot run away from your family. "There are no such things as individuals," the family therapist Carl Whitaker wrote. "Only fragments of families." I have wondered why my parents were not interested in seeing me. Why they didn't want to understand who their daughter really was. In the work I chose, I found purpose, something I was called to do. All I ever wanted was for them to be proud of me.

I stayed in Montana for three years, working first in Great Falls as the coordinator of a parent resource center and then as a childcare worker in a residential treatment facility for abused children on the Northern Cheyenne Reservation. It was a time of tremendous growth, a time when I finally figured out what I was meant to do. In those years I dove deep into my spirituality. I made friendships that enriched me. I immersed myself in the Native culture and exposed myself to things my parents would never know. Could never have imagined.

For a while, I tried to share my experiences with them. I called and wrote letters home. I told them about the kids I was working with and the people I was meeting. I brought them pottery and beadwork, presents from the reservation, and shared stories of the Native culture I had fallen in love with. I wanted desperately to share what I was learning. But even as they listened, I knew they never really understood.

"When are you coming home?" my Grandmother Basili asked one Sunday when she and my grandfather were visiting my parents. After I'd spoken with my mother, she'd handed the telephone to my grandmother. Her gentle voice tugged at my heartstrings across the telephone line.

"I'll be home for Christmas," I'd said, but even as I answered her question, I knew that was not what she was asking.

My choices had consequences. My brother Michael was angry with me for leaving. My parents thought my behavior was selfish. I would miss birthday celebrations, graduations and family dinners. My parents wondered aloud when I would abandon this *thing* I was doing, this exercise in futility. Surely I would come to my senses after I got this out of my system. I would come back home, pick up the thread I had left behind and get back on track. But by then I had ventured too far down the path and with each step I took I veered farther off course. Like the story of Hansel and Gretel from my childhood, the breadcrumbs I'd left behind were gone. I could not find my way back.

On my bookshelf sits a journal I kept in those years. It is filled with the scrawl of a person I hardly remember, someone who ached for acceptance and had not yet grown into the woman I now see each day in the mirror. I hadn't understood the bind I was in and I could not know what the future had in store for me. The struggle I would have to assert my independence. The desire we all have to find our own way in the world. I could not know that to choose what I wanted meant disappointing the people I had always depended on. Only time would tell if I had the strength and courage to forge my own path.

When I graduated from college, my mother wrote an essay in which she talked about the struggles she'd had as she'd watched me grow from the little girl she gave birth to all those years ago. She'd quoted the Lebanese poet Kahlil Gibran, "You are the bows from which your children as living arrows are sent into the world. The archer sees his mark upon the path of the infinite and He bends you with his might that His arrows may go swift and far."

But my mother's dreams were not my dreams.

On a sunny day in June, 1958, Beatrice Marie Basili married Thomas Edward Maggio. She was 21 years old. Shortly after, they moved to New Haven, Connecticut where my father was working on his doctoral degree in organic chemistry at Yale. As I grew I heard stories about those years. They were often repeated when their closest friends gathered together, a group of couples that my parents called 'the brothers' because the husbands had all been members of the fraternity of Pi Kappa Phi back in the days when they all attended Brooklyn Polytechnic Institute.

While my father spent his time doing research and teaching undergraduate students at Yale, my mother worked as a special education teacher. Living on a graduate student's salary wasn't easy and they needed my mother's teaching salary just to make ends meet. Nevertheless, it was a time they remembered fondly. My mother often boasted that despite their meager income, she entertained whenever possible, inviting friends over for dinner as often as they could. She'd make big pots of pasta and they'd drink cocktails made from alcohol my father brought home from the lab. Shorty after my parents moved to New Haven, my mother discovered that she was pregnant.

My mother was 22 when I was born, just a year after they were married. They were the first of their friends to have a child. She left her job at the public school to stay home with me full time. To earn money she began typing theses for the doctoral candidates in my father's program, working after she'd put me down for a nap.

"You were such a good baby," she said. "You never cried. One time, I rolled you out onto the balcony to get some fresh air. It was a cold winter day and I bundled you up, nice and warm, and then I went back to typing. Several hours later (she never actually said how many) I looked up from my work and realized it was snowing. I rushed out to the balcony and there you were, sound asleep under several inches of snow."

My mother loved to tell us stories about our birth, as if she wanted to remind us that we should be grateful for the extraordinary effort she'd made to bring us in to the world. She'd had four kids in four and half years and was living proof that *rhythm*, the then popular Catholic birth control method, didn't actually work. And, it turned out, you could indeed get pregnant while breastfeeding. In March of 1961, a year and seven months after I was born, my brother Michael arrived. While I was born after a long and protracted labor, Michael's birth had been easy. To hear my mother tell it, my brother's head crowned while she was still on her way to the delivery room. His arrival was announced by an African American nurse. "Glory be, it's a head," she proclaimed as she pushed my mother's wheelchair down the hallway.

She'd "almost died" with Elisa, who was born placenta previa in September of 1962, a story that seemed to get worse and worse each time she told it. After Elisa's birth the doctor advised her that she should not have any more children, but less than six months later, she was pregnant again, this time with my youngest brother Robert, who was born in January of 1964.

I found out I was pregnant with Tucker in the spring of 1991. I was thirty-two years old and Bob and I had been married for five years. We lived in a small, two-bedroom house on the westside of Petaluma, a town in northern California. We'd bought a fixer upper, borrowing the down payment from my parents. We spent a year renovating it. We sanded the hardwood floors, re-plastered the walls and replaced most of the windows ourselves. It was a tiny place, but it was home.

I took being pregnant very seriously. I read everything I could get my hands on. Many of my friends had children already, so I leaned on them for advice whenever I could. I stopped drinking alcohol, switched to decaf, modified my exercise routine and made sure I got enough sleep.

My parents came to visit that fall. By then I was six months pregnant and we had already begun to put the nursery together. We borrowed a crib from a friend and stenciled the walls with brightly colored tropical fish.

"Your mother was very excited to see you," my father said as he hugged me hello.

I took their suitcase and led them into house. "You can have our bedroom," I said. "You'll be more comfortable there."

"Where are you going to sleep?" my father asked.

"We'll sleep on the futon in the baby's room," I said.

Shortly after she walked into the house, I saw my mother reach for her cigarettes. "Oh, please don't smoke in the house," I said, stumbling to get out the words. I noticed how nervous I still was settling limits with her. By then my brother Michael had three kids and it was the rule at his house too. Surely she would understand. She gave me a disapproving look and then stepped out onto the porch to have a smoke.

We spent an afternoon together shopping for the nursery. We bought a dresser, bedding for the crib and a fancy new stroller. As we wandered through the department store I was happy she was with me. I wondered if motherhood would bring us closer. It was, after all, something that we could share. I wondered if it would soften the tension between us, the judgment I often felt from her.

That night I grilled some chicken for dinner while my mother made a salad.

"How about some wine?" my father said.

"No wine for me."

"You're not drinking?" my mother asked.

"No, of course not. I'm pregnant."

"That's ridiculous! I drank lab alcohol and smoked cigarettes through my whole pregnancy, and you came out just fine," she said.

I just shook my head.

It wasn't the first time I'd heard that story. She wore it like a badge of honor. In the past I'd laughed, but this time I heard it differently. Her behavior was thoughtless. Selfish, even. But the truth was, it wasn't so much her behavior that bothered me. Maybe things had been different then. Maybe they didn't know what we knew now. But it was her tone that bothered me, the condescending tone she so often spoke to me in, the disapproval I had grown accustomed to.

Perhaps I had been foolish to think things would be different. Perhaps it was too much to imagine that she would have something positive to say. *"Of course,"* she might have said. *"Of course you are not drinking. You want to make sure that the baby stays healthy."* But that was not what she said. Things would not be different. A leopard does not change its spots.

"You may give them your love, but not your thoughts," she wrote, quoting Gibran. "For they have their own thoughts. You may strive to be like them, but seek not to make them like you. For life goes not backward, nor tarries with yesterday."

I wondered if she ever really understood Gibran's words. They'd never come to see me in Montana like some of my roommates' parents had. I'd been disappointed that they didn't want to see where I lived or what I was doing. I wondered why, even now, I still cared.

My mother wanted to see herself as Gibran's archer, launching me, the arrow, into a future filled with my own wishes, hopes and dreams. But there was a disconnect between who she thought she was and how she actually behaved. Instead of embracing them, she'd criticized the paths I'd taken and disparaged the dreams she could not understand. Now, as we stood facing each other, two reflections in the same mirror, she could not accept the part of me that was different from her and I could not accept the part that was the same.

# Chapter 5

# *You are Roman*

I woke to the sun streaming through the windows of the rented apartment just off the Via Aventino. I had forgotten to close the blinds. It was New Year's Day, 2012, and we'd arrived in Rome just a few days before. As the bells of nearby San Saba chimed eight o'clock, I slipped carefully out of bed so as not to wake Bob or my sons who were still sleeping in the next room. I dressed quickly, closed the door behind me and walked down the stairs and out into the brisk January air.

I was a young college student the last time I was in Rome. My life was much simpler then, before the responsibilities of career, marriage and raising children took over. I had taken that time for granted. For years I dreamed of returning. I filled my bookshelves with Italian cookbooks. I bought wine from Montepulciano and began a collection of Deruta pottery. I envied friends who had found their way there. I could not have known that it would take me 30 years to get back to the place that I had loved as a child, but here I was and I wasn't going to waste a single moment.

The streets were empty that morning. The night before we stood with tens of thousands of people along the Appian Way to watch fireworks light up the sky over the Coliseum. Italian rock music blared over rows of loudspeakers and the sound of shattering glass pierced the night air as raucous Romans showered each other with Prosecco and then tossed the empty bottles against the street to explode like rockets.

I walked along the cobblestones and paused in front of a small shrine built into a stone wall that ran along the street. There was a small bouquet of flowers tucked unceremoniously in front of the statue of the Virgin and I imagined an older Italian woman dressed in a black, knee length dress, offering a silent prayer for her family. I turned left at the corner and walked up the hill past the church of San Saba. The wide streets were empty, the shades still drawn on many of the old brick and stone houses. It seemed that everyone was still sleeping.

At the top of the hill, I stumbled upon a long, rectangular, tree lined square in the Piazza Gian Lorenzo Bernini. It was empty, but for three old men sitting quietly in the sunlight, each on their own bench. It was like a photograph I had seen dozens of times in Italian picture books. On the corner, a shopkeeper opened his door for business.

As I walked and soaked in the sunlight, I thought about my mother. I wished she could be here too, the way her parents were the first time I'd come as a young girl. I wished she could have shown her grandsons *her* Rome. But now, she barely remembered the faces of her own children, much less her grandchildren.

I spotted a café and stepped inside. The shopkeeper chatted with a couple who stood at the bar sipping tiny cups of espresso.

"Buongiorno," I said in my best Italian. I wanted to sound native. The sound of my voice broke my trance.

"Auguri," she replied, repeating the greeting Italians used to welcome the New Year.

"Un cappuccino e un cornetto."

She placed the small, croissant-like pastry on a plate and slid it towards me. The espresso machine hissed as she steamed the milk for my coffee.

I ate the pastry quickly, tearing it apart and dunking the pieces into the hot coffee. After I finished, I wandered for a while walking up and down the streets that fed into the square. I felt grateful to be back in Rome after so many years. I let myself take it all in. The sunshine. The chirping of the birds. The rustle of the leaves in the trees. I wanted to wander but I was afraid to get too far from the apartment as I didn't know where I was and I didn't have a map. At the end of the square I started down a short street, ensconced in memories I had not thought about for many years when suddenly I had the urge to stop. As I stood there in the middle of the block, I felt a chill run through my body. I looked up and stared in disbelief at the address of the house in front of me. #5 Via Giacomo della Porta.

I was 12 years old the first time we travelled to Rome. For as long as I could remember, we'd heard stories about my grandfather's sisters who lived there. Over the years they sent letters and Christmas cards. There had even been gold baby bracelets and a set of children's books when we were born, but until that day in 1972, they never seemed real.

My mother wanted desperately to return to Rome. She was two the first time she came with her parents to "Via Giac" as she called it. Her father had come to America as a young man but his sisters still lived in the house where he was raised. She told us stories of playing with her cousins Dino and Lauretta, taking trips to Ostia to visit Zia Wanda, my grandfather's older sister, and many more about the legendary meals served by his younger sister, Zia "B". My mother spoke Italian fluently, learning it as a small child. It had always been her father's intention to return to Rome, but when World War II broke out, it ended his plans to go back to the city he loved.

Her stories of Rome had an ethereal quality, like black and white photographs that had yellowed and softened with age. "You are Roman," she often said. It was a badge of honor. Although Sicilian blood also ran through our veins, it was our family in Rome that she focused on. To my mother, that made us *real* Italians.

She would give to us what her parents had given to her. She would take us to Italy. While my father was willing, he had never traveled out of the country. The planning would be left to her. Long after we had gone to bed, she poured over guidebooks. From my upstairs bedroom, I could hear her tapping on the keys of her blue and white Smith Corona typewriter. This was 1972, long before there were computers or the Internet. She sent letters to hotels via airmail and then waited weeks for a reply. The preparations took months. After dinner, she'd share with us what she had planned, spreading out a map of the city she was working on to trace a route or show us what we would visit. We would start in Rome. We would meet our family. We would see the Vatican, the Pantheon and the Baths of Caracalla; all the things she had seen as a child. After Rome we would travel to Florence and Venice and then later, to Paris, because, in addition to Italian, she also spoke French. It would be her gift to us.

She left nothing to chance. She constructed elaborate itineraries for each day in great detail, listing what we would see and the order in which we would visit. She noted opening and closing times of various churches and museums in order not to miss anything. She carried a copy of *Europe on $5 a Day* everywhere with her, and by the time we left, the pages were bookmarked, annotated and dog-eared. She chose restaurants and learned their specialty of the house. She scheduled time for afternoon naps and to do the homework that we brought along, a promise that she'd made to our teachers when she told them we would be missing the last few weeks of school.

She kept a small spiral notebook and stapled the itinerary to the inside cover. In her tiny, almost illegible scrawl, she kept notes of every day, where we had been and what we had done. She kept track of how much money we spent on meals and souvenirs. While my father took hundreds of photographs, it was the notebooks from those trips that I would want many years later. But Rome was different. She would not plan our time in Rome. That belonged to family. "You will see Rome like real Romans," my mother promised.

She booked two rooms at the Hotel Santa Prisca, a small pensione on the Aventino, one of the seven hills of Rome, one for the four of us and another that she shared with my father. We began each day, each *giornata*, the way the Italians did, by wandering across the street to the bar on the corner. The dark, mahogany counter was packed with people sipping espresso and eating pastry. We filed in after my mother, squeezing into a space at the counter. Zia Nora, one of my grandfather's three sisters and her daughter, Lauretta would meet us there.

"Due espressi e quattro ciocolati," my mother said, ordering for all of us. *Two coffee and four hot chocolate.* I looked into the pastry case and pointed to one that looked like a butterfly all covered in sugar.

I'd been a little overwhelmed the day before when my aunts picked us up from the airport. They'd wrapped their arms around us and kissed us on both cheeks as they spoke to us in rapid fire

Italian. We'd squeezed into my uncle's Fiat and made our way through the crazy Roman traffic. We would have *il pranzo*, lunch, the main meal of the day for Italians, at my great aunt's house before heading to the hotel for a needed afternoon nap.

Zia Nora and Lauretta arrived a few minutes after 9:00. After the traditional greeting of a kiss on both cheeks, my great aunt grabbed my arm and led me across the street, gripping me tightly just above the elbow. Zia Nora was older than my grandfather. She was serious and smart with deep brown eyes and soft white hair. Her voice was confident and strong. My mother told us that she'd been a history professor at the university so we should appreciate how lucky we were to be able to see Rome with her. Zia Nora and I walked arm in arm, the way the Italians did, through the streets of Rome. She bantered back and forth with my mother in Italian as we walked, no doubt catching up on the many years since they had last seen each other. Every now and then, as we stood in front of the Spanish steps or overlooked the banks of the Tiber River, my mother stopped to translate.

Each day, after a morning of sightseeing, we'd return to my aunts' house to eat. The house at #5 Via Giacomo della Porta sat in the middle of a dead end street. The family had lived there for many years and my aunts still leased the modest house from the government the way their father had when he was still alive. It was a two-story structure, a simple stone design, with an arbor covered with bright pink blossoms of bougainvillea. When we arrived for lunch, Zia Bice, my grandfather's youngest sister and my mother's namesake, was waiting for us. She had a kind face with big brown eyes that twinkled when she smiled and above her lip, a whisper of a mustache. Her blue and white polka dot apron was dusted with flour. Shortly thereafter, Zio Dino, my mother's cousin, and his wife

Fernanda arrived along with their two daughters, my second cousins Elisabetta and Paola.

We squeezed in around the large oak table. With so many of us, there was hardly any room to move. We ate pasta carbonara. Roast pork. Grilled eggplant and zucchini. On the sideboard was crostata, a tart made with black cherry jam for dessert. It was all delicious. The room reverberated with Italian conversation. "Mangia, mangia," my great aunts said, encouraging us to eat.

It seemed like we ate for hours. By the time we were done and I stepped outside to jump rope with Elisabetta and Paola, my stomach ached.

> *Piso, pisello*
> *Colore così bello*
> *colore così fino*
> *per Santo Martino*
> *Flat, pea*
> *so beautiful color*
> *such a fine color*
> *for Saint Martin*

The jump roped slapped on the blacktop in rhythm while my cousins sang. They spoke little English and we knew no Italian.

"*Su-san, Su-san,*" they called. Their Italian pronunciation of my name made me smile.

It was my turn to jump.

> *la bella molinara*
> *che monta sulla scala*
> *la scala del pavone*

*la penna del piccione*
*the beautiful lady who works in the mill*
*that mounts on the ladder*
*the peacock's staircase*
*the pigeon's feather*

The sun felt warm against my skin. They began to count. "*Uno, due, tre.*" I jumped in.

*la bella zitella*
*che gioca a piastrella*
*col figlio del Re*
*Toccherebbe precisamente a te*
*the beautiful spinster*
*playing tiles*
*with the son of the King*
*It would be precisely for you*

Surprisingly, all these years later, I still remember the song. Soon, a group of children from the neighborhood began to gather. They wanted to see the *cugini Americani*. As they bantered back and forth, I wished I could understand what they were saying. Why hadn't we spoken Italian at home the way my mother had?

A few weeks later we returned home with a suitcase full of memories. The knot in my stomach I'd felt when I stuck my hand inside the wide stone mouth of the Boca della Verita. Would it, as the legend said, bite my hand off if I'd told a lie? The taste of Zia Bice's cherry crostata. The singsong sound of my cousins' voices as they called my name. *Su-san. Su-san.*

But those weren't the memories my mother wanted me to have.

"Time for a Cardinal Club meeting," she announced one night at dinner. She placed her napkin on top of head. My brothers and sister and I followed suit. My father was away on business and my mother, as she often did when he was gone, took the opportunity to call a meeting to order. "A nickel to whoever can remember the name of the square where we watched the Punch and Judy show."

I couldn't remember. I remembered the show. I remembered the feeling of the sunshine on my shoulders, the laughter of the crowd of children and sitting on the warm pavement. I remembered feeling so grown up and thinking, as I sat there watching the two wooden puppets hit each other with sticks, *I'm too old to be watching a puppet show with all these children.* I was 12 after all.

But I didn't remember the name of the square.

"Pincio," Michael yelled.

"Good!" my mother said. "You win a nickel. And what is the name of the river that runs through Florence?"

Again, I couldn't remember.

"The Arno," my sister answered.

"Correct." My mother smiled broadly. "A nickel for Elisa!" She called the game "It's Your Nickel" and we played it a lot.

I didn't win many nickels.

The thing was, I did remember the puppet show and the walk along the Arno. I remembered climbing to the top of the bell tower in Venice and the picnic we ate that rainy afternoon in Paris. I remembered *all* of it but viscerally, like the wash of color in a Monet painting that soaked into the pores of my skin, not the fine details and specific brush strokes that the others seemed to remember.

What was the matter with me? Why couldn't I remember? With each game we played, I grew more and more discouraged. I felt like a failure.

But something *had* happened on that first trip that would take me years to understand. In those first days spent in Rome, as I walked through the ancient streets arm in arm with my great aunt, jumped rope with my cousins and listened to the church bells ringing as I pulled the covers over my head at night, I began to feel a connection to something much bigger than myself, something I had never felt before. I felt connected to that place and to the people who lived there.

For months after we came home, I thought about my cousins, Elisabetta and Paola. I scribbled their names in my school notebooks. I wondered if they were thinking about me too, their *cugina Americana*. I even imagined changing my name to the Italian, Susanna.

We went to Europe again and again, each time starting our trip in Rome. In college, during my junior year abroad, I brought my friend Missy to "Via Giac." I couldn't wait to introduce her to my Italian family. But it wasn't until I was in graduate school that I began to understand what that first trip had meant to me.

It was a lecture about how our identity, though genetics, behavior and experience, is shaped through the generations. In short, how we carry the histories of the people who had come before. I thought I already recognized the impact of my parents on me, but it had never occurred to me that it also extended to my grandparents and great grandparents as well. It was as if a light bulb went off. I was a part of all of them, of their history. Their experience. No wonder I felt comfortable there. It was where I belonged.

My mother's father, Basilio Basili, rolled his r's and dropped his h's when he spoke. He talked with his hands, pulling his shoulders up towards his ears to emphasis a point. In addition to his pencil thin mustache, he had eyebrows like Groucho Marx. He kept his grey hair cropped flat on the top of his head. He had an athletic build. He'd been a soccer player as a young man and when he got older, dressed in a neatly pressed shirt and tie, his pants pulled high above his waist, he could still skillfully bounce a ball on his head. He was my hero.

I was doing research for an assignment, a paper about my extended family. I needed to understand more about where I came from and how that history had impacted me. I asked my grandfather if he would tell me how he had come to this country. Up until then, the story remained somewhat of a mystery. I had heard that he had been sent by his parents to find his brother who had stolen the family jewels, but as I learned later, that wasn't entirely true. Part of the problem was that my grandfather didn't talk much. In fact, even my mother didn't know the whole story.

Maybe it was because I was the oldest grandchild or because we shared a love for baseball. Maybe I reminded him of my mother of whom he was so proud or maybe it was because I just got lucky, but one afternoon, when my mother and I went to visit, he told me a story I would never forget.

His father, Domenico, worked for the Italian government in the department of foreign affairs. "He was a 'cavalieri,'" my grandfather said proudly. It was the highest position you could hold as a civil servant.

"What did he think about working for Mussolini?" I asked. I had to confess, I was horrified just thinking about it. On the one hand, he seemed to have earned a fairly high position in the government, but on the other hand, I had a hard time imagining my great grandfather working for a man who had allied with Hitler. Was his father a fascist? I didn't dare ask.

Perhaps that was one of the reasons my grandfather had been so reticent to talk about it.

"He made the trains run on time." My grandfather said. If I'd heard that expression once, I'd heard it dozens of times. It seemed to be the thing Italians always said when Mussolini's name came up.

In addition to his three sisters, my grandfather had a younger brother, my uncle Dino, whose real name was Balduino. According to my grandfather, his father, Domenico, was a strict man who demanded that his children go to school and do well but school did not come easily to Balduino and he struggled. In the end, against the wishes of his father, he dropped out.

Domenico worked in the foreign ministry for a man named Ciano, Mussolini's son-in-law. He used his connections to get his son a job on a merchant marine ship sailing to New York. It would be hard work, the kind of job that would surely teach his son a lesson. Domenico hoped it would force his son to go back to school. But, as the story went, when they reached port in New York City, Balduino jumped ship and ran away. His mother was heartbroken. He was her youngest, the baby of the family and he was only 16.

It was at this time that my grandfather, who was in his early 20's, was covering sports for an Italian newspaper. His mother begged him to go find his brother and bring him home so he asked to be assigned to a story that would take him to New York City. There happened to be an international cross country event scheduled, and a team from Italy would be competing. He could cover the race, find his brother and persuade him to go back to Rome. A few months later, in 1926, he boarded a ship bound for New York.

While he was on board, he met my grandmother. She was returning from a trip with her mother and sister to Lipari, an island off the coast of Sicily, where they had gone to visit her mother's family.

"What did you think?" I asked my grandmother who was sitting next to him. She clearly liked this part of the story.

"I thought he was very handsome," she said, her eyes twinkling.

"What happened when you got to New York?" I asked my grandfather. "Did you find your brother?"

"Yes," he said. It hadn't taken long. He was working as a bricklayer for a relative of their mother.

"And did he go back?"

My grandfather shook his head.

Balduino refused to go back and so my grandfather stayed with him. Eventually he and his brother married my grandmother and her sister. My maternal great grandmother bought a two-story brownstone in Brooklyn, on the corner of Maple Street and Rogers Avenue. They all lived together, my grandparents, great aunt and uncle and my maternal great grandmother who we called Nonna. My great aunt and uncle had two children, my Uncle Adrian and Aunt Valerie, and my grandparents, my mother and her brother and sister, Victor and Annamaria.

But I was stunned by his answer. "Never?" I asked in disbelief.

"Not until many years later," he said. "After he was married and had children. But by then mama had died. He never saw her again."

There were a few moments of silence as his words hung in the air. I couldn't understand how bad things could have been for my Uncle Dino to leave home at 16, never to return. He had always seemed so different from my grandfather. He was soft spoken and more reserved. He'd worked as a draftsman for the county, a job my father had gotten him. He wasn't athletic or confident like his brother and as much as I loved him, I hadn't connected with him the way I had with my grandfather. Uncle Dino had broken his mother's heart. Did he feel guilty? Had he regretted leaving? And his mother. I couldn't imagine never seeing your child again.

What I did not recognize at the time was that he too had struggled to individuate. To choose his own path. It was a struggle that begins in adolescence, the journey that every person must embark on to discover who they were meant to be. Who am I? What do I want? What matters to me? These are the questions that shape our identity. But change does not happen in a vacuum. Change for the individual creates change in the system. How will my family respond? Will they create the space I need to explore? Will they be open to what I discover? And will they accept who I become? Now, as I looked at my own struggle to individuate, I saw things differently. I began to understand my great uncle's choices. Perhaps it was all he could think to do.

Thirty years later, I was back in Rome, this time with my own children. My cousins Elisabetta and Paola were married now and Paola had a son of her own. They met us for dinner in a restaurant in Trastevere, just over the Tiber from the center of the city. We reminisced about the days on Via Giacomo over plates of pasta and a few bottles of wine. Although my Italian hadn't gotten any better, both of them now spoke English. There was a lot of laughing and a few tears thinking about the family that was no longer with us. As we left the restaurant, my son Tucker looked at his watch.

"Did you know we were in there for three hours?" he asked.

"Welcome to Rome," I answered.

On our last night, we walked to the Fontana di Trevi, as I had done with my mother all those years ago. The monstrous white fountain in the center of Rome was swarming with people. It was so much bigger than I remembered it. Water cascaded from every side and the enormous blue pool sparkled with hundreds of shiny coins.

As I fished out a few euro to hand to my sons, I thought about that morning walk to Via Giacomo. I had arrived as if by magic, guided by a force deep inside me. I stood there for a long time sorting through my memories. I thought about my mother many miles away. I wished that she could be here, that she might still be able to understand. I finally understood what she'd meant all those years ago. I *am* Roman.

I closed my eyes and let the tears come.

# Chapter 6

# *Connecting the Dots*

I sat on the floor with my back pressed against the window seat in the boys' bedroom. Tucker and Dylan were tucked into their bunk beds, the covers pulled up under their chins. I held the flashlight with one hand and the book with the other. *"Harry woke at five o'clock that next morning and was too excited and nervous to go back to sleep. He got up and pulled on his jeans because he didn't want to walk into the station in his wizard's robes,"*

I read to my children every night, long after they could read for themselves. I loved those moments, when the house was quiet, and the three of us were alone in our imaginations. Each night after I tucked them into bed, I sat on the floor of their bedroom and read by flashlight, invoking the magic of whatever story we shared. *Charlotte's Web. Stuart Little.* The poems of Shel Silverstein. I tried to bring the stories to life, feigning a British accent to be Harry, Ron or Hermione in J.K. Rowling's Harry Potter series. It was as if we were all at Hogwarts, exploring this new world together.

My mother read to us as well. She preferred the childhood classics, like A. A. Milne's *The House at Pooh Corner*, C.S. Lewis' *The Lion the Witch and the Wardrobe* or Dr. Seuss. Books lined the shelves in our house. Of the few memories I have of my very early years, these are some of the most joyful. As we sat together, the four of us flanking her on the couch, we entered an imagined world together, united as one. When we got older she encouraged us to read for ourselves. Like my mother, I loved mysteries. I began with Nancy Drew and then, when I got older, novels by Sue Grafton and Patricia Cornwall became some of my favorites.

I chose to study English literature at Boston College because I did not know what else to do. I wasn't particularly good at science or math. I liked to write and kept a journal of my deepest thoughts and I loved to read. Besides, my mother was an English major. It seemed like a logical choice. But by the time I graduated from college and took my first steps into what would eventually become a career in social work, my degree in English seemed far away from where I was about to go.

Steve Jobs once said, "You can't connect the dots looking forward; you can only connect them looking backwards. So you have to trust that the dots will somehow connect in your future. You have to trust in something; your gut, destiny, life, karma, whatever." When it came to choosing a career, I followed my heart. I did what felt right. I took one step and then another unaware of where my path would lead. There was no master plan. No roadmap I followed. I did not know where I was going nor could I have imagined where I would find myself all these years later. It has taken me many years to make sense of my journey, but now as I look back, I begin to understand how the dots of my own life are connected.

After three years in Montana working with Native children on the Northern Cheyenne Reservation, I made the decision to move to California. I realized I needed more education if I was going to keep doing what I was doing, At the time California had a well-respected and affordable college and university system and Lynn, my former housemate from the Jesuit Volunteer Corps, lived in the San Francisco Bay area. Without too much thought, I moved in with her family and took a job at a residential treatment facility for children who had been abused and neglected and could no longer remain at home.

Clearwater Children's Ranch was situated down a long dirt road in the tiny town of Philo, in northern California's Anderson Valley. I worked as a counselor at Red House, a unit that was the home to 8 pubescent teenagers, four boys and four girls. One night, when I was working the overnight shift, the kids decided that they would sneak out and meet up with some of their friends from another program. Sneaking out was a common activity with the kids in the program. Many of them had been with us for a while, victims of abuse and neglect with little or no contact with their families and a history of running away from home.

A short while later the phone rang. It was Bob, a counselor from Cheetah house.

"I've got your kids," he said. "They were outside trying to recruit my kids to come with them. They were headed into town. I'm on my way back with them now."

"Thanks," I said, appreciative that he was saving me the trouble of going to get them myself. "I owe you a beer."

"I'm going to hold you to that," he said. And the rest, as they say, is history.

A few nights later, we went to the Boonville Lodge, one of a handful of businesses in the tiny northern California town. We played pool and drank beer and within a few months, we were living together. We lived in a 2 room, 44,000 gallon wine barrel overlooking the mouth of the Navarro River. It was a simple, romantic beginning. We didn't have a television and so we spent our time together watching the sun set over the ocean, listening to bands play at the Caspar Inn and taking long walks with my dog, Luke, along the river.

Bob was eight years older than me. He'd moved to northern California from Wisconsin right after college. A credentialed teacher, he liked to joke that I could have been one of the annoying kids he'd taught while doing his student teaching. While his training was in Art education, he was drawn to the kids who other people didn't want to work with, kids who society had given up on. Kids who struggled with addiction, gang violence and the effects of poverty.

My parents met him on a trip to California. They were cordial as they took us out to dinner at the Café Beaujolais in the tiny town of Mendocino, but they weren't shy about sharing their concerns with me. They reminded me that he was too different from me. That he hadn't been exposed to the things I'd been exposed to. They worried he wouldn't make enough money to take care of me. Still, three years later, in the summer of 1986, they hosted our wedding in the middle of a torrential New Jersey thunderstorm that knocked out the power at our reception. If rain on your wedding day brings good luck, we have had plenty of it.

We rented a small house in Fort Bragg, a seaside town in northern California where we both worked as counselors for the local youth service bureau. By then I was in my second year of graduate school on my way to earning a Master's Degree in Social Work. I needed to find a field placement where I could get some experience. I sat at the round marble table in our small rented house, staring at a handful of numbers scrawled on a piece of paper. It was a list of social service agencies to call. I started at the top and began to work my way down.

"Hello," I said, my stomach doing flip flops, "My name is Suzanne. I'm a second year social work student and I'm looking for a place to do a summer field placement."

"I'm sorry," they said. "We usually start internships in the fall. We don't take people in the summer."

"I understand," I said and dialed the next number, but the answer was always the same. After about a half a dozen calls, I grew discouraged. I began to wonder if I was ever going to find someone who was willing to take a chance on me.

I dialed the last number on the list. "Catholic Charities of Marin," the voice on the other end of the line said. "May I help you?"

"May I speak to the Clinical Director?" I said, trying not to sound disheartened.

"That would be Kerby Ann Gleeson." she said. "Just a minute, let me get her for you."

"Good afternoon Ms. Gleeson, My name is Suzanne, I'm a second year social work student," I began again, giving her what by now was my well-rehearsed spiel.

"Sure," came the voice from the other end.

"Sure?" I repeated, surprised.

"Sure," she said again. "We'd be thrilled to have you join us for the summer."

I drove down to meet her the next week. The agency was in San Rafael, almost three hours from where I lived. On the long drive down, I rehearsed the questions I thought she might ask. I made a mental list of experiences that would show my qualification for the position. I hadn't interviewed in a long time and as I sat in the waiting room, my stomach was in knots. I tried to appear calm by thumbing through an old issue of

Good Housekeeping, flipping past articles about *Brightening Your Bathroom in Coastal Blue* and *Five Easy Ways With Leftovers,* but the truth was, I was nervous. Up until then, my experience had been with children, first in the residential programs and most recently in middle and high school. It was "paraprofessional" work, work that could be done without the specialized training of an advanced degree and while I felt confident in that world, I was apprehensive about taking this next step. I began to second guess myself. I'd never worked with adults. I didn't really know much about therapy. Would Ms. Gleeson still want me after she found out how little I really knew?

A few minutes later when the door to the waiting room opened, I breathed a sigh of relief. The clinical director's arms were covered in silver and turquoise that jingled as she reached out to shake my hand. She wore a large beaded medallion around her neck, a white circle with a rose in the middle. She was about my mother's age, with dark hair, eyes and prominent cheekbones. "Welcome," she said. "I'm Kerby Ann." Her office was filled with beautiful photographs, small kachina dolls and beadwork. There were pine cones, shells and feathers. Symbols of her Native heritage. This was too good to be true. I could hardly contain my excitement.

"I used to live in Montana," I said as I introduced myself. "I worked with children on the Northern Cheyenne reservation for a couple of years."

We connected immediately. We shared a love for Montana, for nature and for family. We talked for a few hours. The time flew by. After I drove away, I realized we had hardly spoken about what would be expected of me. Somehow, it didn't seem to matter. I knew I'd landed in the right place.

The agency staff was warm and inviting. They welcomed me with open arms and I immediately felt a kinship with them. Because it was three hours from our home in Ft. Bragg, I spent the summer living again with Lynn, this time sleeping on the floor of the apartment she shared with a roommate in the East Bay. Bob came down on weekends to visit. At the end of the summer, Kerby Ann offered me a job. I would serve as the school counselor for three Catholic elementary schools and see clients for therapy in the afternoons at the agency. It was an easy decision. I went back up to Fort Bragg, packed my things, and a year into our marriage, Bob and I moved to Petaluma, just fifteen miles north of my office. We rented a small house on the westside of town. Bob found a job working as a substance abuse counselor with the local school district. My career as a social worker had officially begun.

Once a week I'd meet with Kerby Ann for supervision. We'd talk about the work I was doing. She'd answer questions I had about what I should do next. In the beginning I was afraid to be vulnerable. Afraid to let her know that I didn't know what I was doing. I sometimes felt like I was pretending. That I was a phony. I worried that I would be discovered, that she would find out that she had made a huge mistake, that I wasn't competent after all. But it never happened.

Each time we sat together, I learned something new. About what it meant to be a social worker addressing the needs of the disenfranchised. To be compassionate and caring and understanding, even when I didn't understand. To listen more and talk less. And to be aware that, even when I thought I did, I didn't know it all. She listened as I shared my experiences. She encouraged me to take risks and she supported me even when I failed. There was never a moment in my training with her when she said *no. No you can't. No you shouldn't. No, it's not possible.* Not once. It was extraordinary.

When I spoke to her, she listened. She cared about what I thought, even when I disagreed with her. She valued my ideas and always was willing to consider them. Despite our difference in age and years of experience, she always treated me with respect.

A few years into my tenure at Catholic Charities, I went home to New Jersey to visit and invited my mother to have lunch. I wanted to talk to her about what had happened with my first love, Chris, all those years ago. We had never spoken about it, and although many years had passed, it still hung heavy in my heart. I hoped that talking about it would help bring us closer and begin to break down the protective wall I'd built between us. I wanted her to hear how hurt I had been and still was. I hoped, like my father, she might apologize.

We chose a small café, just a few blocks from the Somerset County courthouse where my father had been sworn in as a Freeholder many years before. "Mom," I said, after the waitress brought us our salads, "I want you to know how painful that was for me." I spoke slowly and carefully. "I don't think you realize how much it hurt me." But she did not even let me finish my sentence.

"You?" my mother said indignantly. "I hurt you? What about what you did to me?"

I swallowed hard, unsure how to handle what was coming next. I listened while she berated me, rehashing old feelings from that time many years before. *I had hurt her deeply, she said. I had shown no regard for them, for what they'd taught me.* As I sat across from her, a grown woman with a career and husband, I was stunned. I understood she had been disappointed, but it had been a painful time for me too. I had hoped that she would hear me. That the distance might have allowed her to see my side of it. I had hoped that she might be able to hold some compassion for me, her daughter, but I was wrong. Instead, I sat and listened. I did what I had always done. I did not argue. I did not press my point. I stayed silent, choosing to be a good daughter. Deciding, once again to preserve our relationship.

Individuation is the process of becoming one's own person, separate and distinct from their family of origin. To individuate the young adult must claim their place in the world. As she steps beyond the family system in which she was raised, she becomes a separate, independent identity. In turn, the family loosens its grip, softening the boundaries to support the young person as she moves out into the world to find her place in it. She will return again, to introduce the family system to the beauty of her individuated self and expand the family system with the richness she brings with her, the things that matter to her.

But of course to do that requires a shifting of family roles. A mother will always be a mother, but the role that the mother plays to an adult child is much different from the role she plays for her young one. The shifting of roles requires flexibility, a willingness to forgo the old and embrace the new, the way one marvels at the transition from chrysalis to butterfly. The expansion of the family system will enrich everyone involved if they allow it. That's the way it's supposed to work. My mother was many things. Brilliant, creative, dynamic and strong. And yet, when it came to her role as a mother, she was anything but flexible.

I'd gone off to college with my parent's blessing. They'd held the door open for me. I'd begun a career and put myself through graduate school and now I'd come back, changed from the little girl I once was into the woman I had worked so hard to become. I hoped my mother would welcome me, to hold her arms open to me. I'd hoped she would treat me with respect, the kind of respect I felt with friends and colleagues who accepted me for the person I was now. I'd watched this process happen over and over again in my office. Adult children cleared the air and made amends with their parents for things that had happened long ago. Parents and children forgave each other for past hurts and forged different, more expansive relationships. I'd been a part of helping other families achieve that. I wanted it for myself.

But it was not to be. Although I have told this story many times, I am still stunned by my mother's anger, by her need to cling to past hurts and her inability to accept my feelings. I am embarrassed by her emotional limitations. I wish it were not so. As I write this, I make countless excuses for her behavior. I still struggle with a desire to protect her. Perhaps I always will. I've tried hard to understand, but as I sat across the table from her that afternoon, all I wanted was for her to see *me*, to acknowledge *my* feelings, to understand *my* hurt. And when she did not, I wanted to understand why. Although I became expert at recognizing the struggles other families faced and the barriers that kept them from moving forward, I could not recognize those same challenges in my own family. Now that she is gone, I see things more clearly. The truth is, I will never know. She just couldn't.

And so I learned to protect myself. I built a wall so thick she could not reach me. In those moments that we were together, I kept myself safe. I did not share my thoughts or hopes or dreams. I did not tell her that we struggled to pay our bills. I did not tell her when Bob and I argued, when I worried that I wasn't a good enough mother. I did not confess when I lost my patience with my children, when I stayed awake at night feeling guilty. I did not feel safe to do so. And yet I longed for something different. Now, as a mother myself, I understand my role, my part in that aloneness. In protecting myself from her I also kept her from knowing me.

One afternoon, a few years into our tenure together, Kerby Ann said, "I just realized that you are old enough to be my daughter." I hadn't thought about that before, I'd always seen her as my boss. But now, as I look back, I realize that she was a mother to me. In those early years, when I was working so hard to learn this new profession, when I was a new wife and mother, her continual support helped me grow. I never sensed the criticism or judgment that I had from my own mother. Kerby Ann allowed me the space to find my own way. As I continued to come into my own, I modeled myself after her. Later in my career, when I was responsible for the development of other young social workers, I never lost sight of the lessons she taught me.

I sometimes laugh at my younger self. I was young and opinionated. I saw things in black and white. I was quick to judge; myself, others and anything I did not understand. I judged the way I had been taught to judge others. But Kerby Ann was patient. She was my teacher, my boss and my mentor and unlike my mother, over time she became my friend.

I worked for her for almost ten years. During those years at Catholic Charities both my children were born. On days when I didn't have childcare, I brought my babies to work. I set up a small playpen in my office and Kerby Ann and the staff took turns rocking my children to sleep. On my oldest son Tucker's first birthday, they surprised me with a Red Flyer wagon that our executive director assembled late at night after the agency had closed. We were more than co-workers. We were a family.

The years at Catholic Charities were some of the most consequential years of my professional life. They were years filled with firsts, experiences that both scared and excited me. I did lots of things I had never done before but the most significant professionally was my work with families. Family therapy was new to me. In the early years of my career I'd worked one on one with children. I watched as they struggled to make positive changes only to revert back to old patterns after a home visit or reunification with their family. I knew how individual dynamics and personality shaped behavior, but growing up the way I had, in a strong, enmeshed family system, I knew there had to be more.

I wondered why I fell back into old patterns when I was with my own family. Why I still felt like a petulant teenager when I went home. I wondered why I struggled so hard to pull myself away, why my family's love felt like a death grip, a magnet that tugged and tugged, pulling me back to itself. I wondered why I'd struggled so hard in the early years of my marriage. Why so often my allegiance lay with my family of origin over my husband. It all felt like a zero sum game. Individuation from my family felt like death.

I began to study an early pioneer in the field, Dr. James Framo, whose work focused on the idea that beliefs, values and patterns of behavior were passed down from generation to generation. Grandparents to parents. Parents to their children. Left unchecked, they repeated over and over again. I became fascinated with the stories that shaped my clients' lives. Stories about a couple's courtship. The birth of their children. The loss of a loved one. Their stories were filled with heartbreak, joy and wonder. Struggles about loyalty, love and acceptance.

I wanted to understand how the members of the family saw themselves, how the stories my clients told shaped the interactions between them and the possibilities for their future. I was surprised to learn that many of them had never shared their stories with one another. It became clear to me that holding back made it difficult to have the kind of relationship they'd hoped to have. I watched in awe as the families I worked with found their way back to each other, when they discovered that telling their stories allowed for a different connection. And through it all, my own family was never far from my mind.

# Chapter 7

# *One For All*

"You have always been their favorite child." Michael asserted as he looked at Robert. It was a few days after Christmas, 2002, long before any of us knew what was to come. The four of us sat around the large tile table on the back porch of our parents' house on Sanibel Island. The sun was setting and we had just finished dinner. I topped off my wine glass and passed the bottle of my father's Argentinian Malbec to Elisa.

Robert laughed as he shook his head in disbelief. If we'd heard this claim once, we'd heard it a dozen times. Michael seemed to bring it up every time we were together. He sat at the head of the table, the spot my father usually occupied, and leaned back in his chair. "What did you get from Mom and Dad when you graduated college?" he asked, walking us through the evidence, But like any good prosecutor, Michael already knew the answer. We had been having this same conversation for years.

"A camera." I said, playing along. I still remembered the silver and black Canon AE-1 my father gave me when I graduated from Boston College. Photography was my father's hobby, one that he'd learned from his father. My grandfather Maggio had a darkroom in the basement of their brownstone in Brooklyn and when I'd go to visit he'd teach me how to develop pictures. Under the yellow glow of the darkroom light, he dipped the blank sheets of photograph paper into the trays of solution and then we'd watch together as the images appeared.

My father took thousands of pictures. Like his father, he set up a darkroom in the small bathroom in the basement. The closets of our house were filled with trays of slides from vacations in Cape Cod, Lake Sebago and Europe. On Sunday evenings after dinner he would pull out the projector and we'd huddle on the green leather couch in the living room watching hundreds of slides of trips to Italy, Germany and France flash before us on a flimsy portable screen. The four of us posing in the Roman Coliseum. Dressed in red and white dirndls and green leather lederhosen in Heidelberg. Picnicking on ham and baguettes along the roadside in Nice.

We'd celebrated my graduation from college at a restaurant overlooking the Boston harbor. My father reached across the table to hand me a carefully wrapped package. "Congratulations," he said. I was surprised. I wasn't expecting a gift. I unwrapped the package and took the camera out of the box.

"Wow, thanks," I said. "This is really nice."

"Let me help you with that," he said reaching for the box. The camera was in pieces. I heard the lens click as he attached it to the body.

"You're going to have to show me how to use this." I said. My grandfather had given me a "Brownie" for my 12th birthday, a point and shoot camera with square flash bulbs that snapped on to the top of the frame. It was one of the early ones from

Kodak, and a great camera to learn on. The Canon AE-1 was a grown up version, a camera for people like my father who were serious about taking pictures.

My father rarely picked out presents for us. When he did, he'd choose a watch or an occasional piece of jewelry because gifts were my mother purview. One year, he gave me a microscope for Christmas, a not so subtle nudge from my scientist father. But the camera was different. My mother didn't take photographs. That was my father's domain and it began a love of photography that my father and I would share.

"I think I got a camera too," Elisa offered.

Robert chimed in. "Michael, why do we have to do this every time we get together? You know what I got." When he graduated from Yale, my parents bought him a computer.

"And you know what I got?" Michael asked. The question was rhetorical. He had us right where he wanted us. "A beer stein." He paused for a moment and let the evidence hang in the air. "Who gives their kid a beer stein for their college graduation?"

"But it was a crystal beer mug." Elisa added. We were all laughing now.

My mother hovered nearby, her arms crossed against her chest. "And what was in the beer mug, Michael?" she asked, prodding him to continue. Inside the mug was a check. Michael was planning to attend the University of Maryland to earn his Master's Degree in Computer Science. The money was to help him with graduate school.

This was the part of the story Michael always left out, the part that didn't fit his narrative. Was it possible that he really didn't remember? It was true that my parents were proud of Robert who had graduated from not one but two Ivy League schools. He'd been the one who'd done something with all those years of piano lessons, graduating with a PhD in musical composition and working as a composer and university professor. His work fed my mother's love of music and theatre and made her very, very proud.

Like my father, Michael went into business. After graduate school he'd started a tech company that he hoped to sell, but things hadn't always gone as smoothly as he'd planned. He had a wife and three great kids. A beautiful house. He had a good life. Sure, my father had been extraordinarily successful in his career. Still, Michael worked hard and he had a lot to be proud of. I wondered why he felt the need to compete. He had been successful in his own right. I often wondered why he felt so insecure but now, as I looked back I should have known the answer. In our own way we were all still looking for approval. No wonder Michael seemed to be always keeping score. Measuring himself against Robert, he always seemed to come up short.

Over the years, as our families grew and the bedrooms of the house on Sanibel Island filled with grandchildren, I looked forward to the week between Christmas and New Years. Now that we were spread out across the country and had families of our own, we hadn't done a particularly good job of staying in touch. Those evenings after dinner, when the dishes had been washed and the grandchildren were watching television, we often sat around and talked, sometimes with our spouses but also just the four of us, the way we had when we were kids. We'd laugh about the things we'd done and reminisce about growing up together, rehashing stories and old conflicts that somehow never seemed to get resolved. Michael's beer mug story was one of those things.

I hadn't witnessed the partiality that Michael saw. Maybe it was because I was the oldest or because I was out of the house before everyone else. Maybe I believed that my parents loved us all equally. Maybe I just wanted to. They interacted with us differently, but that was to be expected. It wasn't a competition, at least not the way I saw it. I'd seen them go to great lengths to treat us equally. If they'd done something for one of us, they did the same for the other, but maybe that was the problem. The same treatment is not always equal and equal treatment is not always fair. We were different people. We needed different things. Somehow they never seemed to understand that.

We'd grown up a team. Four of us in four and a half years. It couldn't have been easy. By the time my mother was 26, the age I was when I got married, she already had four children. She put us in swim lessons and tennis lessons together. The piano teacher, Mr. Ogren, came precisely at four o'clock every Monday and ran through four, half hour piano lessons. We shared bedrooms and friends. We attended the same elementary, middle and high schools. Had the same teachers. We even got chicken pox and mumps together, a story my mother would share regularly when she felt we needed a reminder of how hard she'd worked to raise us.

Perhaps it was for convenience, but my mother wanted us, expected us to be close. "Friends will come and go, but family is forever," she said. Although I know we must have had fights like most siblings do, I didn't remember many of them. The four of us had our daily chores. I emptied the dishwasher. Michael took out the trash. On Saturday we were expected to help my mother clean the house. We vacuumed and dusted, cleaned our bedrooms and the bathrooms. In the bedroom I shared with Elisa, we had a mirror top vanity covered with dozens of bottles of pastel colored nail polish, purples and yellows and soft baby blue. There were tiny perfume bottles and small glass animals that we bought on a trip to Venice. Although we took turns cleaning it each week, it was a miserable job. You had to take all the tiny bottles off the mirrored top to wipe it down and neither one of us ever wanted to do it. "It's your turn to clean it," I'd command, even when I knew it wasn't.

"I did it last week." Elisa whined. "I'm going to tell, Mom", she'd say turning to stick her tongue out at me.

"Put that back in your mouth before I rip it out," I'd threaten.

In those moments when we argued, I was always the aggressor. I bullied her to get my way and although I never actually tried to rip her tongue out, it never stopped her from believing I would. I could be mean when I wanted to.

But most of the time we got along great. The four of us played ping-pong and pool in the basement and Marco Polo in the swimming pool. We staged annual frog races each summer when we vacationed in Maine on Lake Sebago and when we traveled to Europe as a family, we kept each other awake late into the night laughing as we huddled together in the rooms we shared in the small pensiones of Venice, Florence and Lake Garda. In those early years, we were each other's best friends.

One year, when I was eight years old, my father built us a puppet theatre for Christmas. It was made of plywood, his favorite building material, tall and wide enough for the four of us to stand behind. My mother, who was very creative, sewed a colorful curtain and hung it across the "stage." In the weeks leading up to Christmas, she spent the evenings sewing on her brown and white Singer sewing machine while we were fast asleep in the attic bedrooms above. That year, tucked into each of our stockings, were handmade puppets she crafted out of colored felt, characters from Charles Shultz' *Peanuts*.

The stockings hung in descending order from oldest to youngest. First my father's and then my mother's. Mine,

Michael's, Elisa's and finally Robert's. Although they were in order, I knew immediately which puppet was mine. Lucy, the crabby, know-it-all sister of Charlie Brown peeked out from the top of my stocking. Michael got the very lovable sad sack Charlie Brown. Elisa, the only one of us with curly hair, found Frieda tucked into hers and Robert, the baby of our family, got Linus. We pulled the puppets out of our stockings and my mother directed us to take our places behind the puppet theatre. "C'mon Charlie Brown." we began. "Wake up. It's time to play baseball." We knew the stories by heart.

It wasn't until I had children of my own that I appreciated my mother's efforts. I wanted Tucker and Dylan to be close and I smiled when they played whiffle ball for hours on the front lawn or built Lego structures on the floor of their bedroom. Perhaps not surprisingly, I too devised ways for them to interact. I put a ping pong table and pool table in the garage. I even bought them a puppet theatre. "Friends will come and go, but family is forever," I reminded them.

My mother loved the stories of A.A. Milne. Being an English major, she read to us from the original, Now We Are Six and The House at Pooh Corner. She was our Christopher Robin. One Christmas we found stuffed animals in our Christmas stockings, characters from Winnie the Pooh. Robert, the youngest and smallest, got Piglet. Elisa, who was known to have dozens of imaginary friends, got Rabbit and Michael the wise and worldly Owl. I earned Eeyore. And like the puppets that came before, my mother made them all.

But these were not random assignments. They represented the way my mother saw us and would soon become the way we saw ourselves. I didn't just get Eeyore; I *was* Eeyore, the gloomy, moody, donkey who was always complaining and Lucy, the crabby know-it-all who bossed everyone else around.

In our family, my mother's view was reality. There was no point in arguing with her. And although it made me angry when my brothers and sister would call me "Eeyore" or "Lucy," my mother's perceptions stuck. I would spend the rest of my life struggling to shake them.

I was an extremely sensitive child. Emotions washed over me like a tidal wave. My face hurt from smiling as joy turned into elation. When sadness gripped me, I could not hold back tears. I couldn't just put on a happy face, the way my mother did. I couldn't fake it, I felt things deeply. Tears seemed to come at the worst times. In the middle of a presentation. When I said goodbye to a friend. I cried when I was nervous and I cried when I was sad. I even cried when I was happy. When everyone around me was dry eyed, I couldn't help myself. I took deep breaths. I spoke slowly and carefully. I promised myself I wouldn't cry. But it never worked. My throat tightened. My voice caught and within minutes, the tears always came. It wasn't until I was much older that I realized that there was nothing I could do. There was nothing I needed to do. It was just me. It took courage to be vulnerable. Instead of feeling ashamed or embarrassed, my feelings were something to be proud of.

As children, we each played a role. Michael was the pragmatic one. The oldest boy, he planned to be rich by the time he was forty. "I'm going to buy you a yacht," he promised my mother. Robert, who we all called Bumby, was the youngest. He was cute and funny. He was just our baby brother. He tagged along and adapted to life with three older siblings. He was four and half years younger than me, and it wasn't until I was much older that I really got to know him. Elisa was vulnerable. Unbeknownst to us, she'd been abused by her kindergarten teacher. She began to spend a lot of time alone, retreating to her own protective and sometimes imaginary world. Looking back, her experience had ripple effects for all of us. We grew up with the belief that she was fragile and that it was our job to protect her, but that wasn't true. Elisa was stronger than we knew.

There were three of us in high school at the same time. We played tennis and basketball and ran cross-country, We performed in school plays and went to scout meetings. We spent the hours after school at band practice and theatre rehearsals. We spent Friday nights performing at football games and weekends at band competitions. Because my mother believed in eating dinner together, we often didn't eat until 6 or 7 o'clock, late by my friends' standards. After several years of driving us to and from practice and school my parents bought us a car, a powder blue GMC Pacer and I became the designated driver.

Even in high school, we still hung out together. We spent hours in the basement listening to George Carlin's album AM/FM. We laughed at the forecasts of the Hippy Dippy weatherman '*Tonight's forecast: Dark. Continued mostly dark tonight with widely scattered light in the morning.*' We uttered "The Seven Words You Can't Say on TV," under our breaths, just loud enough so my parents couldn't hear us swearing. We shared friends and even liked the same music. One night we took the train to Madison Square Garden to hear Emerson Lake and Palmer in concert. As we rode in, someone tapped Robert on the shoulder.

"Hey, you wanna buy some pot?"

Robert, who wasn't even shaving yet, didn't bat an eye. "No thanks," he said tapping his front shirt pocket, "I have plenty." It was an indicator of things to come. Robert, whose sense of humor has only grown, was making us laugh even then.

Over the years, our individual differences began to show. We had our own talents, skills and capabilities, but because we followed each other in school so closely, comparisons by teachers were common. While I did well in school, Elisa struggled. After the experience she had in kindergarten, school became challenging. She was distracted and unable to pay attention. There were conferences with teachers, neurological testing and meetings with psychologists to try to figure out what to do. My mother could see she was getting discouraged. One evening at dinner, after yet another meeting with one of Elisa's teachers, my mother called together the Cardinal Club. "What is one thing you don't do very well?" she asked.

It was a strange question. We'd never been encouraged to share our vulnerabilities. It certainly wasn't something my mother believed in. But after Elisa's early experiences in school, my mother became protective of her. She wanted us to shore Elisa up, to make sure she would not feel alone. It was something she hammered home to us. Elisa needed our support. We needed to look out for her and for each other. We were a family. No one would be left behind.

At the time we were all in elementary school. We went around the dinner table and each took a turn. "I'm having a hard time with fractions," I said. While English came easily to me, I was struggling with fifth grade math.

Michael was disorganized and his handwriting was barely legible. My mother, in an effort to help him improve, nicknamed him "The New Neat Michael." He was working on that, he said.

Robert, who, even then, did not lack in confidence said, "I'm not very good at throwing the discus." We laugh about it now, but he wasn't trying to be a smart ass. He was serious. Most things came easily to him. It was the only thing he could think of.

Of all my siblings, I was the closest to Michael. He was only a year behind me in high school and because we were in so many of the same activities, we spent a lot of time together.

There were summers spent working in the county park, he with the maintenance crew and me at the snack bar. The drinking age was 18 back then and in the warm June and July evenings of our college years, we'd go out and hear music together. When he was a freshman at Stonehill College I took the bus from Boston to Easton, about 30 miles away in southeastern Massachusetts. It was Halloween weekend and we dressed up in costumes and went to parties on campus with his friends. We hung out in his dorm room, drinking beer and laughing into the wee hours of the night. In those days he was more than a brother. He was my friend.

But over the years our relationships began to change. Michael lived in Massachusetts. He was married and had three kids of his own. As adults, we grew distant. Those trips to Sanibel were the only time I talked to him anymore. Elisa married and then divorced, left teaching for massage therapy and moved to Santa Fe, only to come back home again and Robert, who came out as gay during his college years was now married with a child of his own. He lived a little over an hour away from my parents with his partner, Tony, and their daughter Annamaria.

As it had been all our lives, it was our parents who continued to bring us together. We had not made the transition from childhood playmates to adult friends the way my mother had hoped. We did not know each other as adults, only as the children we had once been. I did not understand until recently why this was probably inevitable. In a family where we could not be who we really were, how could we possibly have stayed close? Still, on those occasions when we were together, I looked forward to spending time with my siblings and it saddened me that the distance between us kept us from doing it more often.

I could not have imagined how time, spouses, geography and things I had not anticipated would change the dynamic between us.

# Chapter 8

# *The Bottom of the Ninth*

On June 30, 2007, the New York Mets beat the Philadelphia Phillies at Citizen's Bank Park by a score of 8 – 3. Pitcher Jorge Sosa got the win for the Mets. Happ took the loss for the Phils. Paul LoDuca, David Wright and Carlos Beltran went deep for the Metropolitans and Ryan Howard hit one out for Philadelphia. At the All Star break in July, the Mets were in first place in the National League East. By September, however, with three weeks remaining in the season, the team of my childhood would begin a tailspin from which they would not recover. And like the Mets, so too would our family.

I was in New Jersey to celebrate my brother's civil union to his partner Tony. It would be six more years until gay marriage would be legal in the state of New Jersey. On a rainy day in early July, Robert and Tony exchanged vows in front of family and friends along the banks of the Delaware River. By then they had been together for almost two decades. It hadn't been an easy road. My parents had been shocked by my brother's homosexuality, and, like the comments he had once made to me, my father had been cruel when my brother came out to them. His words had hurt Robert deeply, but over the years they had made peace with each other. It had taken time, but my father eventually came to accept my brother and embraced Tony as well. I was proud of him for that. By the time we stood together under the large white tent protected from a mid summer rainfall, Robert and Tony's daughter Annamaria was already 6 years old.

I wrapped my arms around my boys. I had been looking forward to this day for a long time. I was so glad that they were with me, to be a part of this big, crazy extended family celebration. It seemed that weddings and funerals were the only times we were all together anymore. It was one of the real problems with living so far away. I'd grown up surrounded by family; by grandparents and aunts and uncles and cousins. We'd celebrated birthdays and holidays together with platters of antipasti, big plates of pasta and Italian pastries spread out across an extended table where everyone engaged in loud and lively conversation.

But now that I lived in California, holidays often left me disappointed. I'd made efforts to carry on the traditions I'd loved as a child. I cooked some of the foods I'd grown up with, but it just wasn't the same. The house was far too quiet. The table too small. Over the years we'd made an effort to create new traditions. We'd celebrated Easter at the beach in Santa Barbara and spent Thanksgivings in the Sierra foothills. Sometimes we got together with friends, but holidays always fell short of my expectations. I missed my family in those moments and I longed for my children to have the same sense of connection that I had as a child, to feel a part of something bigger. Holidays were about family and mine was too far away. In all the years I've lived in California, I've never really gotten used to it.

Summer was always a busy time for our family. My father and I had summer birthdays, his in June and mine in July. There was Father's Day, and my parents' anniversary. In 2007 my parents would be married 49 years, I would be 48 and my father would be turning 72. If that wasn't enough, the timing of my brother's civil union also coincided with another family tradition, my parents' annual Fourth of July party. Every year they invited the extended family and a handful of their best friends to swim, play bocce and eat my mother's famous sausage and peppers. This would be the first time in years that I would be home to celebrate.

But in late May we received some news that made my visit even more critical. Over the last year, my father had been losing his balance, "flopping" as he called it. My father was a commanding presence. He stood 6' 2, with broad shoulders and thick hands and he was anything but slight. I'd seen him fall several times. At the suggestion of his doctor, he started to go to the gym, riding the bike to strengthen his muscles but despite the physical therapy, nothing seemed to be helping. He'd taken to walking with a cane, just to make sure he could stay steady on his feet. After months and months of testing, the doctors couldn't seem to figure out what was going on.

I stood in the back yard of my California home, gripping the telephone tightly while I steadied myself against the galvanized metal top of my potting bench. It was a beautiful spring day and I'd been gardening when the phone rang, tucking pink and white impatiens into terracotta pots to hang on the back porch. But now I felt weak at the knees, the metal of the garden table hot against my skin. As I listened to the familiar cadence of my father's voice, the air around me became very still, as if the birds had suddenly stopped singing.

"I have some bad news," he said, his voice steady and measured. I took a deep breath and braced myself for what I already suspected was coming. My father had been diagnosed with ALS, amyotrophic lateral sclerosis.

"Are they sure?" I said, but I already knew the answer. Of all the things it could have been, this was, it seemed, the worst possible news. I knew it as Lou Gehrig's disease, named for the New York Yankee's first baseman. Gehrig was a perennial all star, a player who was known for his hitting, part of the famed "Murderers' Row," considered the best baseball lineup in history. But in 1939 at the height of his career, the diagnosis forced him to retire. He died two years later. ALS is a degenerative neurological illness. It would likely progress slowly, my father said, but I knew enough to know that it was fatal. By the time I returned home one month later, this man whose presence had once intimidated me, would already be in a wheelchair.

There are images frozen in my memory. A little girl, standing in front of a black and white television in the dining room of the house on Preston Drive watching a rider-less horse-drawn carriage pull the casket of President John F. Kennedy up Pennsylvania Avenue, the boots flipped backwards in the stirrups. A phone call from my husband early on the morning of September 11, 2001, urging me to turn on the television. Flash bulb moments. Moments that shook my sense of safety the way the 1989 earthquake shook the San Francisco Bay area. For years I've called them "bottom of the ninth moments." In baseball, the bottom half of the ninthe inning is the last chance for the home team to affect the outcome of the game. This was one of those moments.

I flew back to New Jersey with my sons at the end of June. Because summer school had started, Bob, a high school principal, was forced to stay behind. With Robert and Tony's celebration scheduled for July 5th, I wanted us to spend time together, for my children to visit with their grandparents. As luck would have it, the New York Mets, the baseball team I'd rooted for as a child, were in Philadelphia to play the Phillies at the end of June. My brother and sister and I decided to take my parents to the game to celebrate their anniversary and my father's birthday.

I hardly remember a time when baseball wasn't a part of my life. I was eight years old the first time I went to Shea Stadium and the memories of that evening were as fresh as if it were yesterday.

*"Hey, hot dogs here. Get your hot dogs here." The lean, dark skinned vendor rested the big steel hot box up on his shoulder as he climbed up and down the aisles. "Hey, hot dogs hee-ya," he sang, adding another syllable to the word the way New Yorkers often did.*

*It is a warm summer night in June. The crescent moon hangs low in the night sky. Shea Stadium seems enormous. The smell of hot dogs punctuates the thick air and the light stands buzz, washing the outfield in a golden glow. My grandfather unbuttons his suit coat and hangs it over the back of the seat. My brother Michael and I watch the players warm up on the field.*

*It is 1968, the year before the New York Mets win it all. We are the lucky ones. While the others are home with our mother, we are the ones who were chosen to come tonight.*

*"We'll take four," my father said, holding up his fingers just to make sure.*

My father, grandfather, brother Michael and I sat along the first base line in the blue box seats that my grandfather got from his employer, John H. Free. Although he had been a sports writer early in his career, by the time I knew him, my grandfather was making a living selling paper goods. The box seats were used to entertain potential customers.

There were very few sports my grandfather didn't like. As a writer he'd covered track and field events, cross-country races, and soccer matches. He loved the horse races and frequently went to the track. On the night his only son was born, my grandfather was covering a boxing match in Madison Square Garden. It was a story my uncle loved to tell, about how his birth was announced to a crowd of thousands. "Mr. Basili," the PA announcer said to the packed house. "You have a son."

From the moment I stepped into the stadium, I was mesmerized. "Keep your eye on Agee," my grandfather said, pointing to the center fielder. He'd been one of the Mets' hottest hitters, but early in the season he had been hit in the head by a pitch. Now he was really struggling.

I watched my grandfather keep score. I listened intently as he talked to my father. "He's a bum," he'd yell when Jerry Grote struck out. "Come on," he'd call out, tossing his scorecard to the ground when Ed Kranepool missed the tag at first. I loved the way the players' names sounded when he said them in his thick Italian accent. The way he threw his hands up in the air when we left runners on base. My grandfather didn't just watch the game; he participated in it. He sat on the edge of his seat, his sharpened pencil poised on his scorecard. He was all in. Every pitch. Every swing. Every out. When my mother was born, he found an ally. My grandmother didn't care much for sports and so it was my mother who he took with him to sit in the bleachers at Ebbets Field on Saturday afternoons.

New York has always had more than one baseball team, the Yankees, in the American League and the Giants and Dodgers in the National League. The Giants played uptown at the Polo Grounds. My mother's family lived in Brooklyn, not too far from Ebbets field. They rooted for the Dodgers.

My mother and grandfather read the box scores together every morning. She loved Roy Campanella, Pee Wee Reese and Gil Hodges. She'd go to bed at night with the window open just so she could hear the PA announcer's voice as she drifted off to sleep. "Reese to Robinson to Hodges," she'd say, repeating the double play call of her childhood team.

My mother would often share stories about the 'good old days' when the players lived in the neighborhoods and would occasionally be spotted playing stick ball in the streets with the local kids or how sometimes the players' wives would come home with a carload of groceries and the kids would fight to help bring them inside. She said she cried when the Dodgers left Brooklyn in 1957. She had a way of making growing up in Brooklyn seem like an old sepia photograph, all romantic and smoky. I never questioned if her stories were true. They were soft and warm and fuzzy. As I got older I'd find myself getting caught up in her nostalgia, wishing I could step back in time when life, as she portrayed it, seemed so much simpler.

It would be a few years before a new team would come to New York. When the Mets began playing at Shea in 1962, she adopted them as her own. As I grew up, my mother still read the box scores in the paper every morning. Over poached eggs and toast, she taught me about the game. We talked about the hit and run and questioned whether Gil Hodges, the Mets manager, should have let Tom Seaver, his star pitcher, hit for himself in the bottom of the eighth. Baseball, for us, was a talking sport. And, even more importantly, as I grew older, it was the one subject where we could safely approach each other.

When we were kids we'd go to Shea Stadium a couple of times each season. We'd pile in the Country Squire station wagon and drive over the Verrazano-Narrows Bridge, the one that linked Staten Island to Brooklyn. As we drove across the island, through

Brooklyn to Queens, the excitement would build. I'd look for the familiar blue and orange stadium in Flushing Meadows and listen for the sound of jets taking off from nearby LaGuardia airport as they flew high above us. We'd bring our own dinner, stopping at the local Hoagie Hut to get several long submarine sandwiches to share. There was always meatball and one stuffed with Italian meats and my mother's favorite, tuna.

But those were special occasions. Most of the time we watched the games on the television or listened to Ralph Kiner, the Mets' announcer, call the game on the radio, even if it was during dinner. It was the one exception my mother made to her 'no TV at dinner rule,' that and of course, New Year's Day when my father rolled the TV stand into the living room and we ate "buffet style" so we could watch the bowl games. Like her father, my mother always kept score, often penciling in a handmade scorecard on the back of an envelope or on little slips of paper that I'd later find on the coffee table or tucked as a placeholder into whatever book she was currently reading. Like her father, she too was a heckler.

Baseball was in my blood. I followed my mother's lead. The Mets were our team and we wore our loyalty on our sleeves. I hung a blue and orange Mets banner on my bedroom wall. Like my mother, I too had my favorites. Tommy Agee and Cleon Jones, Tom Seaver and Tug McGraw. When the Mets lost, we were heartbroken. When they won, as my mother used to say, "All was right with the world."

"You know what we said when I was a kid," she'd say to ease the sting of yet another losing season, and with the Mets there were plenty of them, "Wait 'til next year." And then she'd look over at my father and smile, crossing her arms the way she did to add an exclamation point before she would inevitably launch into a story about her beloved Brooklyn Dodgers.

I was drawn to the sense of belonging in baseball. The notion that you were all in it together. Baseball depended on all nine guys doing their job. What good was it if the pitcher threw a no hitter if none of his teammates got on base? Rusty Staub might hit a home run to put the Mets ahead, but if Harrelson doesn't turn the double play in the bottom half of the inning, it was all for nothing. Individual accomplishments were nice, but team success was what mattered. If someone fell down, the next guy picked him up.

It was a message that comforted me and felt all too familiar. My mother raised us the same way. My brothers and sister and I may have had our individual talents and strengths, but it was the success of the family that mattered. We were a team. We won and lost together. If one of us succeeded, we all succeeded. If one of us suffered, we shared in that suffering. And like all good managers, it was my mother's job to play to our strengths, to put us in a position to win.

When Tucker was born my mother bought him a New York Mets onesie, complete with a cap and pair of tiny stirrup socks. By then I had long switched my allegiance to the San Francisco Giants, but it mattered little to my mother. Her message was clear. He may not end up being a Mets fan, but there was no question that he would love baseball.

As it turned out that, my kids did love baseball. I hate to think of what would have happened if one or both of them had not been interested in the game. The boys played T-ball and Little League and high school ball. There were gloves and bats for birthdays and Christmas. I celebrated my 30th birthday and most of my early Mothers' Days at Candlestick Park if the Giants were in town, and then more recently at the Giants new ballpark along the San Francisco Bay. I wore my team jersey and brought my glove and I always kept score. And every time

I walked into the stadium, I looked for my mother behind third base.

When everything else was going sideways between my mother and I, baseball remained our safe zone. There were the boyfriends she disapproved of. The decision to do a year of service in Montana. I'd moved to the wrong place. Chosen the wrong husband. Rejected the very things my parents had worked so hard to steer me towards. Over the years, as I began to pull away, when we couldn't seem to agree on anything, we could always talk baseball. Her Mets, my Giants and the kids' Little League teams. It was a place I returned to again and again when I couldn't think of anywhere else to go. In the years when the gap between us seemed more like a chasm, it was the one place I knew where I could find her.

As I drove to the Phillies game, my father and I talked about things we had never talked about before. All of a sudden time no longer seemed infinite. I was eager to learn more about him, to get to know him in a way I hadn't known him before. "What was the best job you ever had?" I'd asked.

"When I was a graduate student at Yale," he said. "I taught some of the undergraduate chemistry courses. I loved that,"

"Really? That was your favorite?" I was surprised. His career had been filled with high-powered jobs. He'd run international chemical companies. He'd travelled the world. He'd made a good living, far more money than I would ever make. He'd had a career in politics. Rubbed elbows with some pretty important people. He'd come a long way from his roots as the son of a postman in Brooklyn.

"Really," he said. "I really liked working with the students. Teaching was fun."

Once we got to the stadium, my brother Robert and I took turns pushing my father's wheelchair up the ramps and settled my parents in the section marked with the blue "handi-capped" sign. It was odd that in all the times I'd gone to games over the years, I'd never noticed that section before. I stepped away to buy a scorecard and then took my seat with the others, just below my parents. I penciled in the lineup.

After I'd finished, I turned to look at my mother and father, just to check in to see how they were doing. They had a lot on their plate these days. Our phone calls over the past year had almost always focused on my father's health, to catch up on his progress in physical therapy or hear about his latest medical appointments. And although my mother's memory issues were more frequent by then, it was still not something we were comfortable talking openly about. We whispered between ourselves and talked to my father when she was out of the room. They had been difficult conversations. My mother was unwilling or unable to acknowledge that anything was wrong and my father was afraid to press. In the few times he had broached the subject with her, she'd become angry.

After the game, as we left the stadium, my mother bent down and examined the large dent along the entire passenger side of their white Chrysler minivan. "Tom," she said. "What happened to the car?"

"Don't you remember," he answered, "You scraped it a few months ago when we were in Florida." As the ALS progressed, my father lost much of the control in his legs. The responsibility for driving now fell to my mother.

"I most certainly did not," she said.

"Yes, you did. You hit that concrete barrier in the parking lot at Costco, remember?" My mother most certainly did not remember.

We drove to Dante and Luigi's, a favorite Italian restaurant in downtown Philly. After dinner, as we got ready to leave, the conversation began again.

"Tom, what happened to the car?"

"Oh for god sakes, Bea," he snapped.

My father was growing increasingly worried about my mother's memory. Along with being forgetful, she became hostile. My sister Elisa, who was living with them at the time, told us she would get angry out of the blue, picking a fight with her or my father. My father was beside himself. He had always been our rock, strong and steady, the one to take care of things, but now he had no idea what to do. There were many nights when Elisa found him, long after my mother had gone to bed, sitting alone in the dark and crying.

Now the game had changed. "Between your mother and me, we're three quarters of one person," he said one evening as we sat alone on the porch. "You have to promise me that you guys will take care of her."

"We will, Dad." I'd said. The starting pitcher would not be able to finish. It would be left to the bullpen to close out the game.

But that was a discussion for another day. Here in the ballpark, surrounded by the smell of hotdogs and freshly cut grass, tomorrow felt like a million miles away. For the time being we were where we had been so many times before, cheering on our favorite team and spending time together.

During the seventh inning stretch, as we stood and sang "Take Me Out to the Ballgame," I turned and faced my parents again. This had always been one of my favorite traditions, a pause in the middle of the game to stretch your legs and enjoy this moment, to sing as one voice and root on the home team. We didn't know it yet, but this was our family's seventh inning stretch too.

Robert and Tony's civil union was a beautiful celebration. My mother and father beamed with pride as they watched them celebrate their love for each other. It had been such a long journey. I was proud of my parents in that moment, grateful that my father had worked so hard to move past his own fears. That he could accept my brother for who he was and I was happy that so many of the people I loved were there.

The next day my father and I sat on the deck of their house on Rockledge Road, the house they had moved to when I was in college. It was a beautiful home tucked in a wooded community on Lake Valhalla, in Montville, New Jersey. The sun streamed through the branches of the maple trees and a yellow finch clung to the perch of one of the many feeders my father hung from the eves of the house. My sister would be here soon to take the boys and me to the airport. It had been a wonderful visit.

"I think you should get some help," I said to him when my mother was out of earshot. We'd been worried about my mother for months, but he'd resisted any suggestions that they needed help. Maybe now, with my father's health compromised, they would finally agree. "I spoke to a social worker at an agency in the area. They said they can have someone come in and help a couple of times a week."

"Your mother will never go for it."

"Dad, I'm worried about you guys. Tell Mom it's for you, that you need help. This is more than the two of you can handle. The woman I spoke to would like to come and meet you. She's going to send you some information. Promise me you'll take a look at it." But even as I said the words, I knew it would never happen. My mother had never been one to ask for help and she sure wasn't about to start now. She was in denial about her own condition and adamant that she could manage my father's too. As strong as my father was, I knew he would never stand up to her.

"Think about it," I said as my sister walked through the front door. It was time to go.

"Thank you," I said, hugging my mother goodbye. She gripped me hard, harder than she usually did when we hugged. When I pulled away from her, I could see that she was crying.

I leaned down and wrapped my arms awkwardly around my father who was still sitting in his chair. "I love you Dad," I said perfunctorily.

"I love you too." The boys said their goodbyes.

I turned to walk towards the door but something made me pause. I turned and looked back at my parents who were still on the porch. I walked back and hugged my father again.

"I love you, Dad," I said again, my words coming this time from a deeper place. I really wanted him to know.

"I love you too, honey," he said.

I turned away before he could see that my eyes were full of tears.

A few days later we were back in California. It was Tuesday, July 10th, the day after my 48th birthday. I got up, made some coffee, dressed and drove to a meeting. After I was finished, I headed home to get the boys to their afternoon baseball practices. Tucker was playing in a travel tournament that weekend. As I steered our green Nissan minivan down the freeway towards home, I checked my voicemail. My brother's voice stung like an arrow shot straight into my heart. "Suzanne," Robert said, his measured tone odd and unusual. "Dad has had a heart attack. It's serious. I'm on my way to the hospital."

I clenched the wheel tightly and struggled to focus on the road in front of me. I began to feel light headed and I couldn't see through the tears that were streaming down my face. I pulled the car over to the side of the road and tried to steady my breath. I felt a scream rise up inside of me, raw and primal, like a volcano. "No." I said over and over. This couldn't be happening. "No. No. No."

My father died almost instantly. At the hospital, my brother found my mother wandering the hallway, confused and in shock. Just five days after returning to California, I was back on a plane to New Jersey, going home.

The pace of those first few days was dizzying. I found myself replaying the hours over and over again. We were just driving to the game together. Just toasting my brother's happiness. Just sitting on the porch and planning for what would come next. I was glad to have been with him. Glad to have had that conversation. I was grateful that I told him I loved him.

It would take me weeks to realize that the heart attack that took his life might have been a blessing. That it saved him, and us, from having to watch the debilitating effects of a horrible disease slowly and painfully strip the life from him. For now I was in shock, waiting for someone to tell me what to do next. I did not know how this chain of events would rock our lives. I could not understand what the promise we made to take care of our mother, the one my siblings and I would remind ourselves of over and over again, would really mean. It was now up to us to close out the game.

But when the closer comes in at the bottom of the ninth, you never really know what is going to happen. In baseball, as in life, the outcome is never guaranteed.

# Chapter 9

# *Bearing Witness*

It was early in the morning and the familiar glow of daylight was not yet visible along the horizon. Most mornings I woke early, around 6 a.m., poured myself a cup of coffee and sat in the silence, taking advantage of the time to think. The dogs, who woke up just long enough to follow me into the kitchen, would soon fall back to sleep on the window seat. The air was still and through the open window I could hear the sound of a rooster crowing in the distance.

But this morning was different. It was Memorial Day weekend, 2010. In a few days Tucker would graduate from high school. It was an important moment for him and for me. Wanting to celebrate it with my family, I'd invited my mother and sister to visit.

"How'd you sleep, Mom?" I said as my mother followed closely behind me. She sat down at the kitchen table, her body wrapped in the bathrobe I'd loaned her the night before. Her dark brown hair was flecked with grey now. She had bags under her eyes. She didn't sleep well anymore. It was hard to believe that my father had been gone for almost three years. At 74 years old, this was the first time she'd been to visit me without him.

"Where am I?" she asked, when I put the cup of coffee down in front of her.

"You're at my house in California, Mom." I said. "You're here for Tucker's graduation. You and Elisa got here yesterday. You're here for a visit."

"Of course." she said, catching herself. She smiled at me and added, "I know."

As Tucker's graduation from high school neared, I wanted my family to be there, to be with us as we marked this moment in his life. Living so far away, I often felt alone and disconnected from the others while they gathered for holidays and family celebrations. I was envious of my friends whose families were present for the big moments in their children's lives; aunts and uncles who helped at birthday parties, grandfathers who cheered in the bleachers at baseball games or grandmothers who busily snapped pictures when the high school couples gathered for the senior prom. Most of our friends had their families around them. I knew their mothers and fathers, their sisters and brothers. For my kids it had always been just the four of us. There'd been no one to babysit. No grandparents to pick them up from school, to take them to the park or out for ice cream. It had just been us. We'd done it alone. I told myself it was the price I paid for living so far away.

It wasn't like my parents never came to visit. Once or twice a year they'd come and spend a few days with us. I spent weeks getting ready. I'd pull out my cookbooks and plan the meals. I stocked the pantry with their favorite foods. I'd take them wine tasting or into San Francisco to see the latest art exhibit at the DeYoung Museum. As much as I appreciated the time I got to spend with them, their visits left me stressed and exhausted. They felt like a performance, months of togetherness compressed into a few short days, days when we put aside our daily lives to entertain them. They lacked the ease that I imagined regular contact—or perhaps a more adult relationship, would have allowed. Although it might sound crazy, I never stopped hoping for a relaxed afternoon chat. A simple cup of coffee on a rainy day. A couple of hours spent sitting in the bleachers at a Little League game.

While my friends' parents had been there for school plays, band concerts and holiday celebrations, my parents missed most of the moments that served as the touchstones of my kids lives. My parents dictated when they would come to visit and I arranged our lives accordingly. Their weekend visits rarely coincided with those important activities but the truth was, I'd never actually invited them. I'd never been very good at asking for what I wanted. It was a pattern I recognized from long ago. I never asked my parents for a new pair of shoes or to go to the movies. I didn't ask for ice cream. None of us had. We waited until it was offered. My parents always did things on their own terms.

Looking back, I wonder what would have happened if I'd invited them to visit? If I'd told them I wanted them to be there for the game or the concert. Would they have come? There had been so many missed opportunities. Instead of asking for what I wanted, I let the moments slip by. I'd let them off the hook. I'd never given them the chance.

Three years after my father's death, our family was still reeling. There had been a host of difficult decisions to make. Relationships were strained and tensions were high. As I thought about Tucker's upcoming graduation, I longed for my family to be there. But Robert was busy with his own family and Michael and I were barely speaking. I wondered if my mother could make the trip.

By then she was living in Lambertville in a small town-house just down the street from my brother Robert. After talking it over with him, I decided to have her come. Elisa would travel with her to minimize her confusion. My sister hadn't been out to visit for a while. My mother's mercurial moods had been hard on her and I hoped the change of scenery might do her good. They would stay for four days. I set up a spare bed in Tucker's room and readied the house for her visit.

As the months of Tucker's senior year ticked by, I often found myself on the verge of tears, set off by the most mundane things. I was dreading the end of this period in my life. In the fall he would be off to college far away from home, and although I was excited for him, I wasn't at all sure I was ready for what was about to come next. I wondered what life would be like without him, when his bedroom at the end of the hall would be empty and the closet bare. While everyone around him seemed to be celebrating this transition, I was increasingly overwhelmed with emotion. I desperately wanted to have someone to share my thoughts with and I hoped that my mother might understand. After all, she'd been through it too. She'd watched four children go off to college. Surely she would understand. I still held out hope that the time together would bring us closer. And although my brother and sister had tried to warn me, I didn't realize just how bad things really were.

But now as I sat across the table from her, I wondered if I had done the right thing.

The night before, I'd heard the hinges on my bedroom door creak. When Dylan was young he would sneak into the bedroom late at night when we were sound asleep. I would hear him open the door and recognize the soft padding of my youngest son's feet as he walked across the carpet. He'd pause for a moment at the foot of the bed and then climb in, tucking himself into the space between Bob and me. Neither of us would say a word. He would just nestle in and drift off to sleep. But that was a long time ago.

Instead, startled from a deep sleep, I woke up to someone standing at the foot of my bed. As I opened my eyes and sat straight up, I tried to orient myself in the pitch black of the bedroom. "What do you need, Mom?" I whispered instinctively, pulling back the covers and climbing out of bed.

Although I could barely make out the contours of her petite silhouette, I could see she was holding something. Draped over her arm were the clothes she had worn that day.

"There's a man in my room," she said.

"A man? Where?" I said. "Show me." I put my arm around her and walked her back to Tucker's bedroom where she and my sister were sleeping.

"Where Mom, where is the man?" I asked again. She pointed to a large, poster-sized photo of Tucker that hung on the wall. He was dressed in his baseball uniform, his crimson hat and jersey, the gold insignia of his high school team clearly visible.

"There," she said. "He's right there."

"That's Tucker," I said. "That's a picture of your grandson." She looked at me, the confusion clearly visible on her face.

"There he is," she said again, turning around and pointing to my sister. Elisa lay on her side with her back to us. She was sound asleep on the air mattress in the corner of the room and she was snoring.

"That's just Elisa," I said. "Let's go back to bed." I took my mother's clothes, hung them on the back of the chair and then helped her back into bed.

"Goodnight, Mom," I said and gave her a kiss on the cheek.

"Is Nana OK?" my husband asked when I climbed back into bed. Instead of calling her Bea or Mom, he called my mother Nana, the way our kids referred to her. I hadn't realized he'd been awake and listening to the whole thing.

"She's OK," I said but I wasn't so sure. I tried to settle myself back to sleep, but I was rattled. I lay awake in the dark for a long time.

The next morning I was on edge, going through my routine with one eye trained on her. It reminded me of the way it was when the kids were little, when I could never let my guard down, never let them out of my sight. I put in a load of laundry while she wandered around the house. She walked from room to room as if she was seeing them for the very first time. After I finished straightening up the kitchen from breakfast, I found her standing in front of the bookshelf in our library, touching the volumes of John Grisham one by one.

"Here Mom," I said, handing her Tucker's high school yearbook. I led her back to the kitchen table and opened it to his senior page to show her the photo montage that I, like the other parents, designed to honor our graduate. There was a picture of him in his letterman's jacket encircled by a collection of photos that represented memories from his childhood. Little League. A family vacation to Boston. A football championship. At the bottom of the page was a quote I had chosen from Thich Nhat Hanh. *'If you look deeply into the palm of your hand, you will see your parents and all generations of your ancestors. All of them are alive in this moment. Each is present in your body. You are the continuation of each of these people.'* I'd hoped it would remind him that we would always be with him.

As she scanned the pictures, I watched for a sign of acknowledgement, a recognition of who and what she was looking at, but it never came. I'd spent hours putting together that tribute for Tucker. I thought back to the newspaper columns she had written for me when I graduated from high school and then college. They had meant so much to me. I had hoped this montage might do the same. I wanted her to appreciate my effort, to acknowledge the sentiment I'd hoped to convey, but she said nothing. Instead, she took her time, moving on from her grandson's pictures to the images to those of Tucker's classmates.

"What do you think, Mom?" I finally said, hoping to coax a response. "Do you like it?"

"Yes," she said, but her words sounded hollow and distant. As much as I should have known not to be disappointed, I'd be lying if I said I wasn't.

I stepped into the laundry room to switch the load of clothes from the washer to the dryer. A few minutes later, I came back to find her smoking, her lit cigarette propped up against the yearbook. "Mom," I snapped, grabbing the book from the table and wiping away the ashes. "You know you can't smoke in my house. Please take your cigarette outside." I rubbed my hand over the cover, hoping that Tucker would not notice the small burn mark in the bottom right corner.

A little while later I looked out the window to see her stooped over, her left hand extended, her eyes trained on the ground. She stopped and reached down to pick something up, putting i t into her outstretched hand. She wandered around the yard, stopping occasionally and then moving on, the way I'd watched her comb the beach for seashells on Sanibel. She'd spend her hours hunched over in what the locals called the "Sanibel Stoop," looking for the perfect coquina or whelk to add to her collection.

"What are you doing Mom?" I asked as I stepped outside. She held out her hand. It was full of tiny colored plastic BBs.

"I've found a lot of these," she said, smiling with pride. "They're all over your lawn."

"I know," I said. "They belong to the kids. They're from their airsoft guns." The guns shot little brightly colored plastic pellets. It was a favorite activity when friends came to visit. "Please don't pick them up."

She smiled at me and shrugged her shoulders. I turned and went back into the house.

A few minutes later she came back in. "Look what I found," she said walking up to Dylan who was doing homework at the kitchen table. She opened her hand and poured the pellets out on the table. "Isn't this great?"

He smiled. "Yes, Nana," he said, his voice hesitating. He was always so kind. He looked at me, confused.

I shook my head. I felt a knot in the pit of my stomach. Her behavior embarrassed me. I wanted her to stop. "Do you want to come with me to take Tucker to graduation practice?" I asked.

"Sure," she said.

As we drove home from the school, I struggled to make small talk. "Are we going home?" she asked.

"Yes," I said.

"It is so nice of you to come to visit," my mother said.

I clenched the steering wheel a little tighter and stared straight ahead. I wasn't sure what to say.

"Your father knew how much I loved California," she continued. "That's why he bought me that beautiful house."

*That beautiful house?* Did she mean my house? I took a long deep breath and let her words wash over me.

In the next few days, I tried to carry on as if everything was normal but it wasn't easy. I felt tense and anxious. I was embarrassed for my mother. I was embarrassed *by* my mother.

I didn't want her to be so sick. I didn't want my children to see her so confused. I watched as she became fixated on things. She searched for the computer she didn't bring. She wandered down the road to buy cigarettes. She accused me of stealing her car. As I lay in bed at night I was overcome with grief. In the months since I last saw her, she had gotten so much worse. In the past she had gone in and out of awareness, but now she was almost always confused. Although Elisa and Robert had tried to warn me, I hadn't really understood.

The next morning she was outside my bedroom door again. "Good morning, Mom," I said. I guided her into the kitchen and poured us a cup of coffee.

"Where am I?" she asked. It was Groundhog Day.

"You're at my house in California," I said, aware of the tension in my voice this time. Why couldn't I be patient? What was the matter with me? I could feel the frustration bubbling up inside. This wasn't the way it was supposed to be. I was angry at my father for dying. Angry that he left us to take care of her. I was angry that my mother couldn't remember. I blamed her for getting sick. I ran through the litany in my head. If only she'd stopped smoking. If only she hadn't drank so much. If only she'd asked for help.

If only things had been different. I wanted things to be different.

Tucker's graduation was outdoors on the campus of the college where I teach. The sun beat down on the rows of plastic folding chairs as the graduates filed into their seats. I had been an emotional wreck all week, crying at the drop of a hat. Today was no different. Tears filled my eyes and I hid behind my sunglasses, a forced smile pasted across my face.

In the days leading up to his graduation I'd found myself looking back, reflecting on so many moments in his life. I couldn't remember what life was like before I had him, before I became a mother. I'd thrown myself headfirst into motherhood and the depth of feelings I had for my children overwhelmed me. There were times I would catch myself watching when they weren't looking, peeking into their bedroom as they played together on the floor. I lingered in the hallway after I kissed them goodnight. I wrapped my arms around them and hugged them tight as if I could squeeze them into me and never let go.

My parents pushed me hard. I too had been guilty of that. I wanted the best for my kids. I wanted them to be successful. I wanted them to be happy. I reveled in their every success and my heart broke when they experienced failure. I hadn't always done the right thing. It hadn't always been easy. I hoped they knew how proud I was of them.

I slid out of my seat and knelt down on the grass, ready to take a picture when Tucker accepted his diploma. I heard the principal call his name and watched as he wrapped my son up in a big bear hug. Tucker and the principal's son Eddy had been best friends all through high school. Tucker was headed off to Cornell for college and to play football for the Big Red, while his friend Eddy would join the Marines. As I watched Tucker walk across the stage, I was overcome with sadness. My children were everything to me. I couldn't imagine life without them. Had my mother felt the same way? Had she ached for me the way I ached for my children? Did she love me the way I loved them?

I introduced my mother to a few of our friends. I stood close by in case she got confused, but surprisingly, she managed just fine. She smiled and carried on conversations with familiar ease. She was always good at playing to the crowd.

Later that afternoon while I ran to the store to pick up a few things for dinner, Bob emptied the dishes from the dishwasher.

"Do you know what time they're serving dinner?" my mother asked.

"In a little while," my husband answered. He ran the dishtowel over the plate and stacked it in the cabinet. "Are you hungry?"

"Oh yes," my mother said. She looked at him curiously. "How long have you worked here? You're doing a very good job."

My husband smiled. "About 23 years."

"You know," she continued, "This is a beautiful club, but the service isn't very good."

A few minutes later I walked into the kitchen and set the bag of groceries on the counter. "Your mother thinks this is a country club," my husband said under his breath.

My parents loved to play golf. Their house on Sanibel sat on the 6th hole of the Beachview golf course, tucked behind a row of ficus trees. Over the years they'd had to replace a few windows from errant golf balls and it was common to see golfers combing their back yard looking for a misplayed shot. They'd taken their turns as president of the men's and women's leagues and collected a few trophies of their own along the way. Of course, no round of golf was complete without a visit to the 19th hole for a gin and tonic or two and a bite to eat, and over the years they'd had plenty of those.

I looked out the front window at the tall maple trees and the green grass, the flowers that circled the lawn. *You mother thinks this is a country club.* Of course she did.

We sat down to dinner at the big oak dining room table. Tomorrow my mother and sister would be heading home. The four days had been difficult, but we'd made it through. Despite how hard it had been, I was glad I'd invited her, glad that she'd been there for Tucker, glad that she'd been there for me. I did not realize it at the time, but it would be the only graduation she would ever see, the last seminal moment she would be present for in either of my children's lives. We held hands and said grace, reciting the prayer we did when we were children. *"Bless us, O' Lord, and these Thy gifts which we are about to receive from Thy bounty, through Christ our Lord, Amen."*

"I'm thankful that we could all be together for Tucker's graduation," I said, continuing. Instead of the rote prayer I'd grown up with, we'd taken to remembering something we were grateful for each day.

"I'm thankful to be here with all of you," my mother said. I squeezed her hand tightly.

"Congratulations, Tucker," we said in unison. We raised our glasses in a toast and then I passed the large platter of grilled chicken around the table.

"You know what I think I'll do when I'm here?" my mother said as she took a piece and put it on her plate.

"What, Mom?" I asked, looking around to make sure that everyone had what they needed.

"I think I'll visit my daughter Suzanne. She lives in California, you know."

# Chapter 10

# *Home*

On a warm evening in June 2003, I sat on the back porch of our new house on Woodward Avenue, just a few miles up the road from the tiny 2 bedroom, one bath house where we had lived for 13 years. We'd outgrown the house on Dana Street. Tucker, now 13 was already six feet tall. I struggled to find new places to put the toys, books and various types of sports equipment in the bedroom he and Dylan shared. We bumped into one another as we lined up to use the single bathroom at the end of the hall.

It was a cool night in the northern California town of Penngrove. The fog had come in from the coast and there was a chill in the air. I was tired. We'd been moving all day. The truck came early that morning to load up what seemed like an enormous amount of stuff. The house on Dana Street was packed to the gills with objects that defined our life together; the finish-it-yourself furniture we bought at the shop that was no longer open on the Boulevard. The table that belonged to my grandmother Basili, its edges worn down in the places wheremy mother and her brother and sister rested their elbows while they ate dinner together. There were cartons of books and boxes of the kids' toys and a kitchen full of toys of my own.

After we unloaded the truck and put the furniture into the new house, I was shocked at how little we actually had. The new house was twice the size of the old one and there were entire rooms that had nothing in them. In the old house the boys shared a bedroom, but in this one they would each have their own. There was a big kitchen and two and half bathrooms and enough space for the boys to play whiffle ball in the yard. We set up the beds in the bedrooms and decided to leave the boxes for another day. We ordered pizza from the restaurant down the street and opened a bottle of wine. That night, as we got ready for bed, Tucker came into my room. "Mom, is it alright if I sleep with Dylan in his room tonight?" In the old house, the boys shared a bunk bed that was now in Dylan's room. We'd bought a brand new full bed for Tucker, one that he'd picked out himself.

"Sure." I said. "Of course you can."

That night I lay in bed and stared at the ceiling. I couldn't sleep. After a while I gave up and walked out onto the deck. I sat down on one of the two Adirondack chairs that we'd bought on a vacation to Victoria, Canada a few years back. There were none of the familiar sounds of the old neighborhood. A car door closing as the neighbor came home late. The noise of the stock car races at the fairgrounds a few miles away. The sound of men's voices after last call at Rays, the local bar. Instead, it was eerily quiet. The moon lit up the night sky and it seemed like there were dozens of stars.

I hoped we'd done the right thing. We were comfortable in the old house. There was a familiarity to it, the way you feel when you slide your feet into a pair of well-worn slippers.

I knew every inch of that house and as small as it was, it was home. Now as I sat there in the darkness, I began to have second thoughts. This house felt strange and foreign. It was a nice house, but it wasn't home. I wondered if it would ever feel that way.

When we bought the house on Dana Street, we spent weeks fixing it up. It was an older house, one that had been ignored for some time, but the moment we saw it, we fell in love. We sanded the floors and plastered the walls. We caulked every new baseboard and replaced every window. It was our first house and we quickly made it our home.

But it was more than that. When I looked around the house on Dana Street, I was surrounded by memories. The birthday parties we'd hosted. The daily chats with the mailman. The scent of wisteria as it bloomed over the arbor in the back yard. The pencil marks on the molding in the boys' bedroom that showed just how tall they'd grown over the years. The house on Dana Street was a part of us. These were the things that made a house a home.

My parents were packrats. Having lived through the Great Depression, they never threw anything out. The closets were full of clothing they no longer wore and old glass coffee carafes from machines they no longer used. There were multi-year subscriptions of National Geographic and Time Magazine and threadbare white 'New Jersey and You' beach towels, no doubt a giveaway at some sort of event my parents attended. They were long past their prime, so thin you could see right through them.

When the last of us left for college, they sold the house we'd grown up in and moved to a house on Lake Valhalla, in Montville, New Jersey. They brought with them many of the objects we'd collected over the years. There were the four twin beds from our attic bedrooms still made with their original coverlets, mine a pink denim weave with blue piping. They furnished the guest rooms on the first floor with items from our childhood. Collections of children's books, of A. A. Milne and Maurice Sendak, filled the shelves. A set of German marionettes hung from the ceiling. On the dresser sat an old owl candle, still covered in the dust collected from years of sitting on my bedroom shelf. I'd bought it the year I had to sell them to raise money for the high school Spanish Honor Society.

There were things they didn't bring. The mint green gerbil cage that sat on my desk, the one that my sister's cat Tigger learned how to open so she could help herself to several of my pet gerbils. The skirted vanity that had been the source of so many arguments between my sister and I. The assortment of posters that hung on the wall, hallmarks of a young girl's childhood crushes and fantasies.

But it seemed like they brought almost everything else.

My marching band letterman's jacket hung in the downstairs closet. In the basement, a large metal street sign, written in Italian. *Senso Unico.* 'One Way.' leaned against the wall, a gift from my parents one summer after a visit to Rome. A rattan peacock chair that sat in the living room of my college apartment on Commonwealth Avenue. *Why did they save this?* I wondered when I stumbled upon them. Their choices seemed odd to me. But like the closet in *The Lion, the Witch and the Wardrobe*, each item unlocked a treasure trove of memories that connected me to the past. The vacation in Heidelberg. The junior prom. The countless halftime performances. Our history was still there.

Although the Montville house was new, the things they brought with them seemed to transfer a sense of home. It was as if each time I came to visit, as I slept in the bed that my great-grandmother once slept in, slid open a closet door to grab a crocheted blanket or flipped through the myriad of photos that filled the bottom drawer of a dresser, I found myself slipping back into a familiar world, one that reminded me who I was and where I had come from. Although it was a house I would never live in, it still felt like home.

In 2007, shortly after my father died, I wandered through the halls of that house. Somehow the slate floors felt less stable under my feet, as if the very foundation had given way. I felt like an astronaut, once tethered to a space capsule, now floating alone in the dark abyss. Attached, I had been free to explore, to go far out into the vast space around me, but now, having lost my mooring, I was scared. I felt lost and vulnerable, as if at any moment I could float away into the darkness.

When Tucker was barely two, my husband and I took him to a park to play. We sat on the bench and watched him discover the world around him. He began to wander, walking off to explore a grassy area just beyond the play structure that up until then had been occupying his attention. I watched anxiously as he walked farther and farther away from us, wondering when he might turn around. *Children will only go as far as they feel comfortable*, I read in one of the myriad of parenting books that sat on my bedside table. *He would eventually turn around, I thought. Wouldn't he?* When he was 20 yards away he turned to look at us, smiling a big toothy grin. Buoyed by the safety of knowing we were still there, he turned around and continued. I jumped up from the bench and ran after him.

Now, many years later, I thought about that moment. At the time I hadn't given much thought to the two of us sitting on that bench. I was focused on Tucker, on making sure he was safe. I worried that the books were wrong, that he would never turn around, that he would wander off unaware of the dangers that he could face. But Tucker knew we were there and our presence, the emotional tether that had given him the confidence to explore. We were there if he needed us, ready to catch him if he fell.

But now it was me who was wandering and for the first time I realized there was no longer a need to look back. The bench was empty. There was no one to catch me. The man who once sat there was gone and the woman who sat beside him was like a wraith fading in and out of existence.

The day after my father's funeral, we gathered on the porch of my parents' house. My siblings and I had to think about what was next. How we would take care of our mother now that our father was gone. As we stood in the same room, alone for the first time that weekend, it felt strange even as it felt familiar. My father's absence loomed large. I wondered where to start.

"What are we going to do?" I said. "She can't stay here alone."

"She can come to Lambertville and stay with us for a while." Robert said, taking charge. "It will give us time to figure out what's next."

"I'll pay her bills," Michael said. He had a gravely voice and mumbled when he spoke and I found his rapid speech confusing. It was as if he never had time to slow down, to really connect. Over the years he dove deeply into his own family, rarely having time for the rest of us. He was like my mother that way, building a wall around his own nuclear family. Still, I was touched when he asked me to be his daughter's godmother. A few years later, I asked him to be Dylan's. Although I sent gifts to his children for their birthdays, he always seemed to forget mine. Sometimes I wondered if he even cared about us at all. I was hurt that he had pulled away and I did not understand why he acted the way he did. It never occurred to me that his idea of family might be different from mine.

While we were standing around trying to figure out what to do next, Michael was growing impatient. He and his family planned to drive back to their home in Massachusetts. He seemed eager to finish the conversation and I was growing frustrated. I wanted him to stay longer, to help us figure out what to do. I couldn't help but feel like he was abandoning us in our hour of need. I expected our father's death would bring us together, to bind us the way we were when we were kids, but I was wrong. Clearly he did not see things the way I did. After a while he went down to my father's office. He grabbed my parents' checkbook, my father's computer and whatever bills he could find, said his goodbyes and walked out the door.

Elisa and I went up to my parents' bedroom. Eager to ease my mother's sadness, we began to clean out my father's belongings, as if removing his clothes would help my mother forget that she had just lost her husband. Stepping into the bedroom, it was as if he was still there. His clothes were draped over the chair in the corner, his watch on the top of his dresser. Even the air smelled like him, a mixture of stale cigar smoke and cologne.

As I walked towards the closet, my eye was drawn to the blue dress shirt draped over the chair by the bed. Wasn't that the shirt he'd worn just the week before at Robert's civil union? The last time I was with him? Elisa and I worked in silence. While she emptied out his dresser, I stepped into the closet and began mindlessly stuffing clothes into big black garbage bags. As I rifled through the shelves, my hand landed on a small wooden cigar box, one of many my father had lying around the house.

I always hated that my parents smoked. In our house, the smell of cigarette smoke was a constant, like my mother's White Linen perfume or pasta sauce simmering on the stove.

As kids we tried to get my mother to quit. We'd thrown out her cigarettes and begged her to stop, but she would just get angry. My father smoked cigars after a nice dinner or while on vacation, or when he worked on his ship models in the garage. Cigars, my father convinced us, were not the same thing as my mother's cigarettes. For him, smoking was an occasional thing, not the two-pack-a day habit my mother had.

I picked up the box and opened the lid. Inside were several small Swiss army knives, corporate giveaways, no doubt. A handful of golf tees and a leather billfold imprinted with the words Dynamit Nobel, the chemical company he had retired from just 10 years earlier. I put the box aside. I would take it home with me.

The next day Bob and Tucker flew home to California. Bob would take Tucker to a baseball tournament while the rest of us took my mother to the Jersey shore. We needed to get her out of the house, to give her a change of scenery. As we walked along the Seaside boardwalk, I held my mother's hand. I couldn't remember the last time I'd done that. The lively sound of arcade games and the chatter of children were a stark contrast to the silence between us. My mother seemed so fragile. For the first time I noticed that her vibrant brown eyes had begun to fade and a thin grey ring had settled around them. She had always been such a formidable opponent, someone who commanded a room, but as we walked along it was as if a gust of wind might blow her away.

We stepped into Maruca's Pizzeria and found a table in the back. Tony ordered a few pies and we tried to make small talk, anything to distract us from what was going on. We kept the subjects light and no one dared mention my father. We didn't want to cause her more pain. "Try and eat something, Mom," I coaxed, the way I did when my kids were little. I slid a slice of pizza towards her. It was piled high with sausage, mushrooms and an assortment of vegetables. "Grandpa would hate this pizza." I said, trying to fill the space.

"Why?" someone asked.

"Because Grandpa believed that pizza should be simple," I said. "Grandpa liked pizza the way the Romans ate it, with a topping or two, not with all this stuff." I pointed to the piles of olives, peppers and onions. "Isn't that right, Mom?" My mother smiled. We'd had that conversation many years before, when her parents were still alive and living in a retirement community in Maryland. I wondered if she remembered. It seemed like such a long time ago.

We spoke in fits and starts. We focused on the pizza. On my niece, Annamaria. On the weather. Anything to avoid talking about the only thing any of us was thinking about. Each time there was a lull in the conversation, panic set in. I was afraid of the silence. Afraid of the sadness. I struggled with what to say. I wondered what came next, if anyone would fill the void, but somehow, someone always did.

We were a team. In the coming months we would surely be leaning on each other as we figured out what to do next. I thought back to that promise we had made to my father just the week before. It was a conversation we would return to again and again. Did he know what was coming? Had he understood what he was asking of us? We had a big job ahead of us. As we sat together, huddled in the back of the pizzeria, I was thankful to have come from such a big family, to have my siblings by my side.

My mother went to live with my brother Robert temporarily. It was clear we couldn't leave her in the house alone. In the days after his death, the house in Montville became eerily quiet. I would come up the stairs to find her standing in the entryway, smoking a cigarette and staring off into the distance. I wondered if she understood what had just happened. She seemed so lost, her body so frail. The soft bronzed skin that once exuded the warmth of the sun felt cold to the touch. I remembered listening to her footsteps in the house on Preston Drive, the powerful click of her heals against the hardwood floors, but now her feet barely made a sound. As she walked across the tile floor, her soles no longer made a mark.

Over the years, when I'd gone back to visit, I'd sleep in a downstairs bedroom at the end of the hall, a small dark room furnished with an ornate, dark cherry bedroom set that once belonged to my father's maternal grandmother. At night I would lie in the bed and listen to the sound of my parents' feet on the floor above me. I heard their voices as they wished each other goodnight. It did not matter how long I had been gone. Each time I came to visit, I found myself drifting back. I was 7 or 12 or 15, tumbling backward in time, swallowed up by the familiar. I returned to a world I knew all too well, a world that had once defined me. In those moments, I was home. But now the house seemed vacant. The life sucked away. Without my father it no longer felt like home.

Eight months after my father died, my brother Robert helped my mother buy a small townhouse on Delevan Street, right around the corner from his home in Lambertville, New Jersey. She'd be moving to a small townhouse with less than half the space of her old home. We put my parents' home on the market and when it sold, Robert hired a family friend to clean out the house and sort through her belongs. What we couldn't fit in the townhouse we would place in storage to sort through later.

I was too far away to help and the task was enormous. Every square inch of the house in Montville was filled with the things they had collected over the years. There were decades of accumulation. Rooms of furniture. Closets filled with boxes of slides and photo albums from trips to Europe. Thousands of books, a baby grand piano and my father's N gauge train set that filled the room just off the garage. Since none of us would be there, my brother assured me that he had given his friend instructions to save what seemed important. We rented a dumpster and he got to work. By the time he was done, all that remained from their 49 years of life together was packed into cardboard boxes.

"What is he throwing out?" I asked my brother more than once. It bothered me that this person I did not know had been left to decide what to save. How did he know what was important to us?

"What do you want to save?" my brother asked, but the truth was, I didn't know. I couldn't remember what was there. Like my mother's memory, it felt like the life that I knew was slipping away and I was too far away to do anything about it.

The townhouse in Lambertville was nice enough. Robert and Tony moved my mother in. They rented a storage unit and filled it with whatever couldn't fit in my mother's new home. They tried to make it comfortable, surrounding her with the things that she needed. They hung photos on the walls to remind her of the people she loved. They set up her bedroom with the big queen bed she had shared with my father. The bed that was now half empty.

But the house on Delevan Street never felt like home. The homes my parents lived in reflected their personalities. My mother never had great taste. There had been a green leather couch paired with orange upholstered chairs, a faux fur rug and rattan sectional, mismatched styles and conflicting colors, but they were all her. This space was all wrong. These were not the choices she would have made. Although some of the belongings were familiar, the gestalt was off. Like the dementia that had begun to erase her, any sense of my mother was missing and the absence of my father loomed large.

Her memory was far worse than any of us had known. Neighbors found her wandering the streets of Lambertville and called my brother to come and get her. She put aluminum foil in the microwave and left lit cigarettes burning around the house. She fought violently with my sister and became increasingly suspicious. She accused me of stealing her car, a 20 year old Lexus that once belonged to my father. After a car accident totaled my minivan, we'd had it shipped out to California with her blessing, but she could never remember. Although it sat in the garage for years, she told everyone who would listen that I had stolen it.

We hired caregivers to come in each day. There was Marie, the kind gentle senior who took my mother to the theatre. Rhea, the young social worker who chronicled every minute she spent with her. There was Bonnie and Gwen and Sheila. They took her shopping and out to lunch. We arranged for Meals on Wheels to drop off food for her each day because left to her own devices, she would forget to eat. But every step we took was met with resistance.

At times it all seemed unmanageable.

After a year or so, my brother Robert began to talk about finding a place for her to live. He was concerned about her isolation. He was worried that she wasn't safe. It was taking a toll on his family. My sister too, was struggling. As my mother's memory got worse, her aggression and paranoia grew. My mother screamed at her caregivers. She locked them out of the house. She sent them home. She didn't need help, she said. She called me continually, pleading with me to send them away.

"There is a strange woman in my house," she said to me one day.

"What woman?" I asked.

"This woman. She is sitting on my couch right now. She is demanding that I serve her lunch. She is eating all of my food. You must make her leave."

"Mom," I said. "That's Gwen. She's there to help you."

"I don't need help," my mother snapped. "I want you to send her home."

I vacillated between compassion and despair. She would not admit she needed help and although I tried hard to understand, I grew annoyed by her resistance and angered by the constant opposition to everything we tried to do for her. How could I help her if she refused to acknowledge what was going on? She was nasty, hostile and at times aggressive. Why did she have to make everything so difficult? My siblings and I were only trying to help, but no matter how many ways we approached it, it was always the same. She fought us every step of the way.

"Don't you dare speak to me that way," she chastised. And so I backed off. Despite all her challenges, she was still my mother.

I tried just to listen, to use the skills that served me well as a social worker. Although they worked with my clients, they failed me time and time again with my mother. I tried to be understanding. I struggled to be patient. At times I was forceful. "I will not send her home, Mom," I said, trying to take charge, but that didn't work either. Frustrated, I complained to my siblings. At least we had each other.

I tried to remind myself that it was the disease, that she couldn't help herself. But the truth was, there was a way in which her hostility felt all too familiar. Perhaps if it had been unusual I might have been able to be more compassionate. I might have been able to let her anger roll off me without penetrating my skin. But the truth was, I'd been through this before. Like a cut that begins to fester, her words found their way in, binding to wounds that already existed and although my head told me not to take her behavior personally, my heart knew differently.

Now as I look back, I wonder how different things might have been if she could have admitted what was going on. If she'd let us help her. Had she been aware of what was happening? As she found herself confused and forgetful, was she frightened? When my father was diagnosed with ALS, he went into it with his eyes wide open. He did research. He talked to us about what was happening. He told us what to expect. But my mother had been different. She did not talk about the challenges she was having. She never told us she was scared. She never asked us for help. She did not have the courage to be vulnerable with us. I wonder what might have happened if she had.

Again and again my brother tried to persuade me to move her to a facility. Still I resisted. I wanted her to be surrounded by the things she knew. I did hours of research and talked to friends and colleagues, people I knew with expertise in dementia. I worried it was too soon, that removing her from the things that were familiar would make things worse for her. I wanted to keep her in her own home as long as we could and I felt bound by the promise I made to my father.

But within three years we would put that house on the market too. My mother would go to live in a locked dementia unit in the back of an assisted living facility in a town she would never know the name of. We packed the things we wanted to save in more cardboard boxes and put them into the storage unit.

One Saturday afternoon we held a yard sale. Dozens of strangers traipsed through my mother's house, scouring the tables for bargains. "This is cute." a young woman said as she rifled through a box and held up a gold plated wreath decorated with a partridge, a couple of turtle doves and three French hens.

"My mother loves The Twelve Days of Christmas," I said.

Christmas was always her favorite time of year. The annual Christmas party that she and my father hosted was a much sought after invitation, a perennial red circle date on the December calendar. There was Christmas punch and rum soaked fruitcake, piping hot beef stroganoff with long grain rice and the requisite singing of carols that signaled that dinner was near.

My father wore a Santa Hat and a silver whistle and conducted the ceremonial singing with a thin strand of spaghetti. He was a master at getting people to cooperate, even if they didn't really want to, and the threat of not being fed was a powerful motivator. The highlight of the evening was the singing of *The Twelve Days of Christmas*. Their guests drew tiny slips of paper that separated them into singing groups. The Three French Hens and Four Calling Birds and the Eight Maids a Milking found their partners and gathered together. The singers had to perform their parts to perfection, lest the conductor signal the need to start again. From the beginning.

The drawing of the parts was always random, except, that is, for the partridges. The whispers began as soon as the slips of paper were opened. The partridges, on the other hand, were selected ahead of time. Those slips of paper were handed secretively to a chosen few. The role of the partridges always went to my father and his college fraternity brothers from Pi Kappa Phi. Sometimes their guests rebelled and tried to upset my mother's well-oiled plan but it never worked. My mother always had the final say. Despite some good-natured teasing and a few well timed and less than noble efforts at bribery, tradition always held. My father and his fraternity brothers always sang the partridge part.

We were expected to help her get ready. We cleaned the house. We lay out cocktail napkins and polished the silver. When the guests arrived we welcomed them and took their coats. We passed out hors d'oeuvres; pickled herring, sweet and sour hot dogs and hot clam dip. After our chores were done we retreated to the basement. The Christmas party, while fun for the guests, was just work for us.

In preparation for the yard sale, we'd sifted and sorted through the life that was once ours. The souvenirs from trips to Europe. The 1st grade class photos and baby books and years of birthday cards. My father's Republican elephant collection, their trunks raised in victory, and the countless Waterford Crystal vases that held my mother's prized zinnias and snapdragons and pale purple lilacs. It was all there. My mother would never return to her own home. It was time to move on. Time to let go of many of the things that had marked her life, their life and ours, together.

One by one, they walked out the door, those pieces of history. They were carried out by strangers who did not know that they walked out with a little piece of each of us. The leather carafe from Florence. The glass plate from Murano. The silver butter dish that I polished religiously each year for the annual Christmas party. These were the talismans of our life together.

It took six months for our house in Penngrove to finally feel like home. Until Bob, Tucker Dylan and I moved in, I hadn't thought much about how a house became a home. I think I'd always taken it for granted.

That Christmas I hung the stockings over the fireplace and set up my grandfather's nativity scene on the side table.

We decorated the tree and set out my small collection of nut-crackers on the top of the buffet. By now the rooms were filled with furniture. I wandered the hallways without turning on a light. Despite having a bedroom of his own, Tucker was still sleeping in the bunk bed with his brother. Shadow, our black Australian Shepherd, found a favorite spot on the window seat. As I went off to work each morning, I looked forward to returning home. I now felt grounded here, embraced by the quiet, the dappled morning sunlight that poured through the trees and the smell of honeysuckle in the air. It seemed that when I wasn't paying attention, we'd been busy living. Now I understood that more than the belongings that surrounded us, it was the life that we lived that made a house a home.

On the day we were to move my mother to her new home, my brother and I drove her to the assisted living facility. It was a late summer day, three years since my father's passing. There was an awkward silence in the car. I wondered if Robert felt as guilty as I did. I worried that we had failed her and the promise I made to my father hung heavy in my heart. As we walked her into the foyer and handed her over to a complete stranger, I tried hard to push aside the feelings of regret that washed over me and yet, I knew there was nothing else we could do. We had tried everything we could think of. We had held on as long as we could. But now we had finally come to the realization that someone else could do a better job of caring for her than we could.

She would share a room with a woman we did not know. It was a tiny space, with a bed, a nightstand, a dresser and a small closet. We hung a few paintings on the wall and placed photos of my father and the four of us on her dresser. We hung her clothes in the closet and laid a comforter on the foot of her bed. It wasn't much, but we tried to make it home.

Here we were, dropping her off like Paddington, the bear found perched on his suitcase in the famed London train station. *Tied 'round his neck, a small tag of instructions. "Please look after this bear," it said to whomever might find him, "Thank you."* The words came back to me as the social worker met us at the door, a knot of anxiety planted firmly in my stomach. We were the grown-ups. It was all on our shoulders now. Were we prepared for what was to come? How would we navigate an unfamiliar sea?

"Please look after this bear," I whispered as I handed my mother over to a stranger. *Please look after this bear.*

# Chapter 11

# *Alone*

In the fall of 2006, a crisis was on the horizon.

I stood in the doorway to my office and looked around the empty room. Nails poked through the walls where pictures once hung. Gone were the photos from the staff retreat and the collection of heart shaped rocks that sat on my desk, gifts from former students I'd trained over the years. In the parking lot, my green Nissan minivan was loaded with memories of more than 20 years of a career in social work. As I drove away from the Family Institute of Marin for the last time, my eyes filled with tears. I'd been running the struggling mental health nonprofit for almost 10 years. I had a dozen staff and a handful of volunteers. We did good work, providing mental health services to kids and their families but we weren't the only game in town. We were in constant competition for funding with larger agencies, and even in a wealthy county like Marin, resources were hard to come by.

That same year, an American economic crisis was also brewing. Big banks and financial institutions played loose and fast with other people's money. Subprime mortgages were being handed out like candy and the economy would soon be in trouble. Within twelve months the mortgage industry would tank, foreclosures grow and the country would be mired in the biggest financial crash since the Great Depression. It became nearly impossible to secure enough money to keep going.

I shut the doors to the agency just as things were growing bleak. I was 47 years old. Bob and I had two children, a home and dozens of bills to pay and for the first time in my life, I was unemployed with no prospects on the horizon.

Soon after, the economy crashed. Although my husband was still working as the principal of a continuation high school, we needed both our incomes. It didn't take long for us to get under water. Managing the finances had always been my job. I juggled the bills as best I could but there was never enough. I alternated payments, paying the water bill one month and then not paying it the next. I ran up our credit cards, not sure how I would make even the minimum payments. Each month I held my breath and waited for the next paycheck to come. I managed to make our mortgage thanks to a small severance package and an equity line we'd taken out years before, but by the spring of 2007 that too was depleted. We fell behind. One month and then another. My stomach was in knots each time I sat down to pay the bills. The stress was overwhelming. It was hard to sleep. I left bank statements unopened. I was afraid to answer the phone. Like an ostrich, I tried to bury my head in the sand. And then the bank threatened to foreclose on us.

I continued to apply for jobs. I took a part time job teaching at a culinary school. We applied to modify our loan, but the bank was taking forever. Still, the phone calls and foreclosure notices continued to come. For months I kept hoping that something would break but by the summer of 2007, I still had not found consistent work and we were in deep trouble. Something had to change. Embarrassed, but without any other options, I decided to call my father and ask for help.

He had helped us in the past. As my grandfather had once done for him, he loaned us the money for the down payment on our first home. But there were no freebies where my father was concerned. If we borrowed money, we were expected to repay it, with interest. He wanted to teach us financial responsibility, he said. And so we made a schedule and paid him monthly until we'd paid back every penny.

It had been many years since I'd needed his help. I'd always had an uncomfortable relationship with money. I envied my brothers who seemed to have their financial lives in order. To me, there was never enough. We did not live extravagantly. We did not take expensive vacations. And although we managed to make things work, we had no savings and every bit of the money we earned went towards our bills. I prided myself on being independent and although things hadn't been easy, we somehow managed. But by the summer of 2007, all that changed. As much as I hated to have to ask my father for help, we were desperate. I had no other choice. I would swallow my pride and make the call. I couldn't think of anything else to do.

But then my father was diagnosed with ALS. The early part of the summer was spent dealing with his diagnosis and a month later, celebrating Robert and Tony's civil union in early July. The timing just wasn't right. I would wait until I returned to California, but before I mustered up enough courage to make the call, my father died.

When we returned home from the funeral, there was a note on our door. After months of threatening, the bank began foreclosure. In a panic, I called my brother. "Michael," I said, my voice betraying the fear I felt, "We are in trouble. I need to borrow some money from Mom." I explained our situation, my voice quivering through the tears. Michael had agreed to manage our mother's finances. As embarrassed as I was to ask my younger brother for help, I had no other choice. I had to keep my house.

He listened carefully. "It's going to be OK," he said. "We'll figure it out."

I breathed a sigh of relief. "Thank you," I said.

Michael promised to speak to our mother. My parents had always said yes in the past, and I hoped to buy some time to allow the bank to modify our mortgage. Still, my mother was struggling to cope with my father's death. She had been in shock and almost catatonic the last time I saw her and yet I convinced myself she would understand.

Shortly thereafter, Michael wired the money to the mortgage company. We set up a plan to pay her back with interest. The bank modified our mortgage and we managed to keep our house.

The truth was, I should have known better. My mother wasn't in a place to make a decision and yet, it was a matter of survival. I couldn't lose my house.

A month later my brother Robert called. He'd just learned about the loan. "You don't have a right to do that without talking to all of us," he said, his voice harsh.

I struggled to explain. "You're right," I said. "I'm sorry." It was hard enough to talk to Michael. I hadn't told the others. I had always felt so vulnerable when it came to money and the truth was, I was filled with shame. I was worried that they might say no and I couldn't take that risk.

"I'm sorry," I repeated. "I'm going to pay it back. Every penny."

"That's not the point. We have to stay together. You needed to come to all of us. We have a right to know."

I hung up the phone, shaken and filled with guilt. In the past few years my brother and I had grown close. I hated letting him down. Robert's tone had been sharp and judgmental. His anger all too familiar. In that moment he reminded me of my father. I felt alone and cut off from the very people I needed the most. As much as I resisted my father's help, I always knew he would be there if I needed him. He was my safety net. But now I wondered where I could turn? Who, if anyone, could I count on?

"It's not our money," my brother had said. Of course he was right. We had a responsibility to my mother. We agreed to set some ground rules. Information would be shared. Decisions would be jointly made. There'd be no more borrowing of Mom's money. We had to work together. It was the only way we were going to get through this.

Two years later, Bob and I were still trying to dig ourselves out of a deep financial hole. We made our payments on the loan to my mother but money was very tight. I took on two jobs, teaching and working at a local homeless shelter. The boys were now in high school. I'd insisted on sending them to private school, adding tuition to an already stretched budget. It wasn't the soundest financial decision and there were many reasons not to, but like my parents I believed that education was important, a gift that I could give my children. I wanted them to have what I'd had. And like my parents', I hoped a smaller, Catholic school environment would benefit them, that it would prove to offer them opportunities they might not get at the much larger public school. Bob reluctantly agreed.

I was slow to understand the hole created by my father's death or the impact it would have on our family system. Up until then, the structure was clear. There was never any question who was in charge. My father was our foundation and our security net. He provided the frame on which my mother built the house. It was she who set the rules. She who held the boundaries. She who decided who was in and who was out. My mother kept us nestled together. She shaped our views and molded our personalities. As we grew older we would return, again and again, to the house that they built always knowing where we fit in. We gathered at their invitation. We folded back into the structure. We played our part.

But now the structure we had come to depend on was gone. The foundation shattered. My mother struggled just to carry on a conversation. She could no longer identify the day or month or year. The woman who had once done the New York Times crossword puzzle in ink could barely spell her name. Now, she spent her days sitting at a small table threading plastic beads onto nylon string. It was just the four of us left. It was all on our shoulders now. It was up to us to hold the family together. To discover what, if anything remained.

When we divvied up the responsibilities that day on my mother's porch, I did not understand that the family structure had shifted. Although we had not made it explicit, I believed we would work together, united by the promise we'd made to my father. I imagined we would stick together but it soon became evident that I was wrong.

Robert, Elisa and I took turns managing her day-to-day life. We communicated regularly. Group emails filled my inbox. We were constantly on the phone, checking in with one another and asking for advice. In the years after my father's death, we sold two houses and bought her another. We spent hours dealing with doctors and caregivers. We fought to have her evaluated. We weathered her hostility and although I could hardly afford it, I flew back and forth to the East coast every three months so I could sit beside her and hold her hand.

But Michael's approach was different. Rather than working with us, he managed his end alone, sending us sporadic updates now and then. There were no phone calls, no chance to check in and say hello. When his emails came they were brief and to the point. He did not reach out or try to stay connected. And although we tried to keep him in the loop, the infrequency of his communication made that difficult. I soon found myself hurt and angry.

Within months of my father's death, he'd all but disappeared from the rest of us. He rarely visited my mother or called to check on how she was doing. Two years before, when I'd gone to him for help, I'd felt a connection that reminded me of the way we'd been when we were younger. I'd hoped it would continue. Now, more than ever, we needed him to be with us. To share the daunting responsibility of taking care of our mother but he was nowhere to be found.

The truth was, Michael began to distance himself from us many years before. Although he may have had his reasons, he never shared them with me. I did not understand why he stayed away. He was my brother and I loved him. I often wondered if he spent as much time thinking about us as we did about him.

The loss of my father prompted a seismic shift in the family. We always understood what was expected of us, but suddenly it was no longer clear. The family, or what was left of it, began to feel fractured as if we were spinning in a centrifuge, thrown out into space. Soon, cracks began to fester. In the next few years there were a multitude of struggles. Decisions that threatened our sense of connection. Choices made that we did not understand. As we stumbled to make our way through crisis after crisis, there were plenty of hard conversations. Harsh words whispered under our breath when no one was listening. Sometimes we grew frustrated with one another. Often we felt off balance. There were nights when I lay in bed and stared at the ceiling, my thoughts swirling around me. I felt sorry for myself. I blamed my father for dying, for not letting us know how bad things were with our mother. I was angry that he had left us alone to deal with this.

"Do you ever get mad at Dad?" I asked Robert one day.

"Yes," he said. I breathed a sigh of relief. I was glad I wasn't the only one.

Sometimes it felt like it was all too much, when the responsibility hung like an albatross around my neck. The decisions were all ours now. There was no one else to make the hard choices. When Elisa lost the home she was renting in a fire, she moved in with my mother. We made the decision to let her live rent-free while she got back on her feet in return for caring for our mother. But Elisa struggled and living with our mother proved to be very difficult. As her dementia worsened, she became more and more hostile. Elisa's efforts to support her were rebuked. My mother grew violent. She was defensive and scared. As much as Elisa tried not to, it was hard not to take things personally. My mother railed at my sister and often brought her to tears. Looking back, I don't know how Elisa survived.

In the years that followed, there were months when Michael and I didn't speak to one another, when I wondered if we would ever find our way back to the comforting harbor we once knew. I took for granted the relationships we had as children. We'd been so close growing up. Although our lives had taken us in different directions, I counted on that closeness to get us through these difficult times. I'd blindly trusted the bonds that once held us together, but I'd been wrong. We were in new territory now, a system fighting for survival. Instead of a team, it was each man for himself. We formed temporary co-alitions that often became strained and broke apart. I became frustrated with my siblings and they, in turn, disappointed with me. As I struggled to make sense of what was happening, I began to wonder if what I remembered had been true at all. Had we been as close as I'd once believed? Where was the loyalty to our family? Where was our commitment to each other?

And yet, somehow we muddled through, bound by the vow we'd made. We repeated it as though it was a mantra. It shone like a beacon in the darkest of nights, a lighthouse that signaled shelter in a stormy sea. As fractured as things became, we continued to come back to the one thing we always agreed on, the promise to take care of our mother.

# Chapter 12

# *Opening*

Although my mother's death might have seemed like the end of my longing to connect with her, it was instead, an opening I could not have anticipated.

It was Monday and my mother had been dead for three days. The McDonough funeral home felt claustrophobic. It was warm inside, a stark contrast to the biting cold of that January morning. As I dressed for what I expected to be a difficult day, I prepared myself to meet the family and friends that would come to say goodbye.

In the funeral home, people milled about, speaking in hushed tones. In the front of the room, my mother's ashes lay in a small, wooden box surrounded by sprays of tropical flowers, a nod to the life she had loved on Sanibel Island. A group of cousins gathered around a montage of photos we pulled together the night before, photos from trips to Europe, backyard barbecues and walks on the beach. "Where was this taken?" I heard someone say, but I didn't hear the answer. The days since my mother's death had been a blur.

Phone calls. Appointments. Decisions. Someone tapped me on the shoulder. I turned to find my sister Elisa, standing with two women I did not recognize.

"We're so sorry about your mom," one said. She reached out to give me a hug.

"Thank you," I said and forced a smile.

"I don't know if you remember me," the other one said. "My name is Linda. Joanne and I worked with your mother."

"Oh sure," I lied. "Of course, I remember you." Their names drifted into the air around me, never quite landing on my ears.

For most of my early childhood, my mother had been a stay at home mom. After the four of us went to school, she started writing a twice weekly column for the Home News, a central New Jersey newspaper. She spent the second part of her career in public service. It turns out that supporting my father in his political career had helped her make a few connections of her own. Shortly after I left to go to Montana to begin my work with the Jesuit Volunteer Corps, Judge B. Thomas Leahy, the presiding judge of the Youth and Family Division of the Somerset County Superior court, appointed my mother coordinator of a new Youth Services Commission. The commission brought together local government and community agencies to address the needs of at-risk youth. Like my father, Judge Leahy had been a freeholder and he'd known my mother for years.

At the time, I wondered why he had chosen her. She had no formal experience in program development or social work. Other than writing her column, and a short stint as a teacher before I was born, my mother's experience had all been gained through countless years of volunteer work, through the PTA, the Women's Club, and of course years of campaigning.

"Your mother was a dynamo," Linda said. She had taken over the coordinator's position after my mother retired. She ran through a list of accomplishments in my mother's tenure.

I tried to listen politely, but found it hard to focus on the conversation. I scanned the room intermittently, looking for familiar faces. My father's brother and his wife, my Uncle Phil and Aunt Margie. Paul, my father's fraternity brother, and his wife, Jean. They had been friends with my parents since their college days. Uncle Vic, my mother's brother. I felt myself floating, disconnected from my body.

"Probably the thing we were the proudest of was Megan's Law," Linda continued.

Megan's Law? The words snapped me back into focus. Megan's Law was something I knew all too well, both as a parent and a seasoned social worker. It was a federal law that required local authorities to identify the names of registered sex offenders to the public. It was named after Megan Kanka, a 7 year old New Jersey girl who was murdered by a neighbor convicted of sex offense. The law was first drafted and passed in the New Jersey State Assembly and then adopted by the federal government shortly thereafter. My mother had been appointed to the committee that wrote the original legislation by New Jersey Governor Christine Todd Whitman. She collaborated with people from all across the state. Had I known this? It turned out that over the years my mother had been part of some significant legislation.

"She was so proud of you." Joanne said. She smiled as she placed her hand on my shoulder. "She used to gather us together in her office and tell us about what you were doing. We'd hear about the programs you were starting, about your work in Montana on the reservation. She'd say, 'I want us to do that,' and then we'd have to figure out how."

I nodded politely as they continued, a forced half-smile plastered on my face, but the truth was, I had no idea what they were talking about. *She told them about what I was doing?* My mother never seemed particularly interested in the work I did. *What could she possibly have wanted to replicate?*

"Who were those women we were talking to at the funeral home?" I asked Elisa later that night. I had forgotten their names already.

"You mean Linda and Joanne?" As my mother's illness progressed, Elisa stayed in touch with them.

"I guess that was them. They said Mom used to talk to them about the work I was doing. What were they talking about?"

She shrugged. "I have no idea. They've said things like that to me too."

It all seemed so surreal and I hardly believed it. They hadn't been specific and I hadn't asked, but now I wondered what they had meant.

I knew my mother's work with the county had been important to her. I remembered times when she would tell me about what she was doing, but I have to confess, I found it hard to listen. She had a tendency to name-drop. Her stories often included the names of people I didn't know, judges, state officials and even the governor. It always felt like bragging. Why, I wondered. Was she trying to impress me? I didn't care. Instead it just made me angry.

For years I struggled to get out from under her shadow, to find my own path. In social work, I finally discovered something that was just mine, separate from her. But now, like most things between us, this too began to feel like a competition. With every story I shared, she countered with a story of her own. Why did it always have to be about her? I just wanted her to listen when I spoke. To respect what I was doing. But as I listened to her recount her accomplishments, it felt like she was taking this away from me too.

And of course she was wildly successful. Less than a year into her tenure with the county, she was chosen "Woman of the Year." By then even her coworkers understood her competitive nature. At the dinner honoring her achievement, her staff got together and performed a song they had written based on a tune from the old Rogers and Hammerstein musical, *Annie Get Your Gun.* They called it "Anything You Can Do, Bea Can Do Better." Evidently I was not the only one who felt that way.

Although I did not know it at the time, the seeds of my social work career were planted in the mountains of Appalachia, many years before when I was still in college. While I had been raised Catholic, my understanding of religion was rote and disconnected from my day to day life, something saved for Sundays and holy days. The service trip to Georgia introduced me to social justice work, a concept much different from the volunteer work I had done in the past. I soon came to understand that social justice work was a way of *practicing* the faith I was raised in. After we returned from our trip, I went to hear speakers who had dedicated their lives to serving others. I took a volunteer position at an after school program in East Boston. I attended mass, not on Sunday morning in the big, sanitized church of my childhood, but late at night, sitting on the steps of Shaw House, an old building on Boston College's upper campus, surrounded by people I loved. We took turns reading, not just from the Bible but from other books that mattered. Writers I had never heard of; Thomas Merton, Henry Nouwen and Matthew Fox. I wanted more.

My roommate Missy had a sister who had joined the Peace Corps and was teaching in a small African village in Lesotho.

Although I had already committed to graduate school, I could not deny that the thought of joining the Peace Corps sounded exciting to me. One afternoon I filled out an application. Soon thereafter, I took the T, Boston's metro train, downtown to interview, but a few months later, when the acceptance letter came with an assignment to Togo, I was too afraid to follow through. Looking back, I wish I'd had the courage to go.

I had a friend who joined the Jesuit Volunteer Corps after graduation and now worked in an AIDS clinic in San Francisco. It was a year long term, a lot shorter than the more than two years the Peace Corps required. JVC focused on four core values: community, simple living, social justice and spirituality. Volunteers committed to working with the poor and disenfranchised to make a difference in the lives of others. They would be assigned to local non-profit organizations. The Corps would provide shared housing and cover living expenses. Volunteers would live in community and in return, would receive a stipend of $50 a month.

Of course none of this mattered to my parents who still did not understand why I had chosen this over graduate school. After that phone call when they'd reacted so angrily to the news, we had mostly avoided the subject. In early August I drove out to Spokane, Washington with a couple of friends to begin my JVC orientation and training at Gonzaga University with several hundred volunteers from all across the country who would be sent to communities in Alaska, Washington, and Montana.

I was assigned to Great Falls, Montana. We were seven women, strangers from places like Wisconsin, New York, Michigan and California, and we were part of a larger group of Montana volunteers. After a week of training we began the drive to western Montana in yet another old Country Squire station wagon, this time in greenish blue. In addition to Great

Falls, there were communities in Hays, Ashland and St. Ignatius. While my housemates would work in a domestic violence shelter and a teen parent program, I was assigned to work at St. Thomas Children's Center, an organization run by the Sisters of Providence.

Housed in an old, multistory brick building in downtown Great Falls, St. Thomas had once been an orphanage. Now, in addition to a residence for elderly nuns, it was a children's center for the community. I would be responsible for creating a parent resource center, a place that would provide information to the parents of the families in the daycare as well as the community at large. I'd never been responsible for starting a program before. I was as green as they come but what I lacked in experience, I made up for in enthusiasm. I couldn't wait to begin. I had no idea what was in store for me, but as was true for the other 6 women that would become my community, what happened that year changed my life.

Sister Susan was around forty, I guessed, with flecks of grey in her short thick hair and a dimple when she smiled. Her appearance had surprised me. The nuns I'd had in high school had been covered from head to toe in the traditional habit, but Sister Susan wore a dark blue pantsuit. Her head was uncovered. If it wasn't for the large silver cross that hung around her neck, I might not have even known she was a nun. She was from Washington and had a strange, Northwestern accent that was foreign to my New Jersey ear. She was one of a handful of nuns we met that year. I'd grown up with a strict, traditional view of religious men and women. Most of the nuns I'd known had taken their vows with male names, like Aloysius, Edward and James. My relationships with them had been formal, and the notion of addressing them as anything other than "Sister" was incomprehensible. I'd once gotten detention in high school for just forgetting to add "Sister" to the end of my affirmative response when I'd been asked to move over during band rehearsal. But unlike the nuns I'd had in high school, these women were approachable and friendly and our relationships, while always respectful, were warm and affectionate.

The building was cavernous, with high ceilings and long corridors. At the end of each hallway was a statue of a saint that towered above, with eyes that seemed to follow you as you passed by. Sister Susan directed me to a large room, a former dining hall I guessed, that had been divided with partitions into smaller office spaces. She introduced me to a couple of women huddled over a large conference table and then showed me to my desk. "Let me know if there is anything you need," she said. And with that, she left me there.

In the beginning, I had no idea what I was doing. I sat at my desk and shuffled papers around, trying to look busy. I forced myself to make phone calls to people I did not know, to introduce myself and see if I could meet with them to gather information and learn about the resources in my new community. It was awkward at first, but gradually, over the next few months I found my footing. I gathered information and created a manual full of resources for problems I had never even thought about. Child Abuse. Domestic Violence. Drug Addiction. I learned just enough to be able to speak coherently about these topics. I did interviews and wrote articles for the local paper. Once, when I was invited to be a guest on a local television show to talk about child abuse prevention, I sent the tape of the show to my parents. In a discussion with the host about parenting styles, I happened to mention that I had been spanked as a child.

"You just told everyone that we abused you." My mother said one day on the phone.

"I did not. We were talking about discipline." Parenting practices were changing, I'd told the interviewer. What worked when I was young was not acceptable anymore. In the interview I'd used my own childhood as a reference for how things were different. But my explanation to my parents fell on deaf ears. For months, every time they mentioned the video, it was characterized as "the time Suzanne told everyone that we abused her." I just rolled my eyes.

It turns out, I wasn't cut out for program development. I hated working alone. I didn't like the feeling of being disconnected. I found the work boring and I wondered if it even mattered. When I couldn't stay in my chair anymore I'd go downstairs to work in the day care with my housemate Cathie. Working with the children felt more real somehow. The children were full of energy. They rushed me when I entered, wrapping their arms around my legs to hug me. They bounced off the walls like pinballs of excitement. I did whatever they needed. I ladled bowls of chicken and dumplings. I cut hundreds of slips of colored paper. I read *The Cat in the Hat* until I was sure I could recite it by heart. Cathie and I even started a Campfire Club.

Like my family had done, my housemates and I ate meals together each night. We spent hours sitting at the table, talking about the things we were learning. Lynn, Terah and Marilyn, worked at Mercy Home, a shelter for victims of domestic violence. One afternoon they were asked to transport a woman back to her house so that she could get some clothes.

"Call the police before you go," their boss advised.

"The police?" Lynn asked. It seemed simple enough. They would just drive her home to pick up a few things and they'd be back within the hour.

"Yes," their boss answered. "Her husband has a shotgun and he's driving around town looking for her."

"A shotgun?" I repeated. I couldn't even imagine. And that, of course, was the point. There were many stories like this one; about women who had been victims of violence. Children whose parents struggled to put food on the table. The struggles of a teenage mother who was barely old enough to drive. These were stories I had never considered, far away from anything I had ever known. And yet now, as I listened to the stories each night, for the first time, I began to understand life differently. I felt myself expanding, as if a part of me cracked open, a place where new seeds of compassion might take root. These were stories of pain, heartbreak and struggle and my heart ached for the people who were experiencing them.

But there was also something else, something that was not as obvious and harder for me to see. With every story of struggle came moments of strength, courage, and resilience. The courage of the mother who left her home in the middle of the night because she wanted her children to grow up in a place where they were safe. The dedication of the 16 year old who stayed up late to do homework long after she put her infant to bed. The young Coast Guard father who listened patiently as his daughter showed him the drawing she had done, even though he was exhausted after spending the night guarding a missile silo and wanted nothing more than to go home and rest. Over time, my heartache turned to awe.

The work we were doing forced me to think about things I had never even considered. I had grown up in a middle class, white, homogeneous neighborhood. There'd always been enough money. There was always enough to eat. What struggles we had were nothing compared to what I was seeing. I had been raised to believe in middle class values. That we alone are responsible for our own destiny. That hard work led to success. I didn't know anything about privilege, systemic racism or oppression, all concepts that, after years of working as a social worker, are so familiar to me now. I didn't know it at the time, but I had a lot to learn.

And as challenging as the work was, the hardest thing that year was the self reflection I was forced to do in order to live in community. Up until that time, my experience living with people I did not know was limited to my freshman year in college when I was paired with a prissy roommate from Florida who got up at the crack of dawn to begin a two hour makeup and hair routine, one that contrasted dramatically with my tendency to jump out of bed and throw on a pair of sweats as I ran out the door. Most mornings I barely remembered to brush my teeth. Our relationship had been a disaster. We never got along. After months of trying to work it out, we just stopped talking to one another. In college it had been fairly easy to work around my roommate. The dorm was full of other people to choose from. But this was different. We were seven strangers who had committed to building a community, not just sharing a house. As I would soon find out, I had no idea what that meant.

We lived in a mustard yellow one-story house on the Northwest side of town. We lived as a family. We had a joint checking account and one checkbook. We drove an old station wagon. We ate meals together and took turns doing the shopping, cooking and cleaning. There were five bedrooms and seven of us. Marilyn, who was starting a second year of service, already had a room. That left 4 to choose from.

"I'd like my own room," I said timidly. I had shared a room all my life. Surely I *deserved* my own space. I scanned the room waiting for someone to object.

"I don't mind sharing," Lynn said.

"Me too." The others said. I pushed away my embarrassment.

Lynn and Terah took a bedroom in the basement. Darra and Chris would share the one at the end of the hall. That left Cathie and me with our own rooms. I'd gotten my wish. A few minutes later, I dragged my suitcase down the stairs.

Every Wednesday night we had a house meeting. It was the time to talk through any problems we might be having and try to resolve them. They were long and sometimes tedious, and if I'm being honest, I rarely looked forward to them.

One night, after dinner, I grabbed a cup of tea and met the others in the living room.

"I think we need to talk about the grocery budget," Darra said. "I think we should buy more things that are generic."

"Like what?" I asked.

"Like toilet paper."

I know. This sounds like a stupid thing to have to talk about. At least I thought it was and it soon became a bone of contention between us. We didn't agree, or I should say, *I* didn't agree. I had never bought a generic anything in my entire life and I wasn't inclined to start. Generic was for *other* people, for people who couldn't afford the *real* thing. I was as sure of that as I was about anything. The week before, when it had been my turn to shop, I bought Scott Tissue like my mother did. Now evidently, there was a problem with that. I felt criticized. Judged. Discounted. I was angry. I shot back.

"It's *toilet* paper," I said, emphasizing the ridiculousness of it all. I was not about to give in.

My roommates listened. "We promised to live simply," they reminded me. It was true. It was part of our commitment. *To live simply so that others may simply live.*

I was unmoved. I argued back. They listened. Two hours later, the meeting was over. I had lost the fight. I went down to my room and sulked.

The thing was, it wasn't really about toilet paper. I didn't understand it at the time, but I learned something that day and many of the days that followed. I grew up believing there was one right way. I witnessed my parents' ridicule other ways to do things. They were right, everyone else was always wrong. I'd lived a privileged life. I'd been spared the choices that many of the people I now worked and lived with made. Until I lived with these women, I hadn't had to stretch too far outside my comfort zone. As much as I fought against some of the rules of my own family, at least I understood them. But now I'd made a commitment to live in community with people who were raised differently than me. Who valued different things and had different ideas. Wrong and right no longer seemed clear. I'd promised to be part of this community, even when it wasn't easy. I couldn't walk away.

Over time I began to understand. I had work to do. I needed to learn how to listen to others even when I didn't agree. I needed to let go of the belief that there was only one way. Of needing to be right. I needed to do things I had never done before. And yes, I might even need to buy generic.

When I'd found out I was going to Montana, I was excited to be surrounded by the Native culture. My knowledge was limited, gained from the books I'd read and the movies I'd seen. Over that year I visited the Crow, Ft. Belnap and Northern Cheyenne reservations. I quickly became awed by the pageantry, the culture and the traditions of Native life. I liked it so much that after a year in Great Falls I went to work on the St. Labre Mission in Ashland, on the Northern Cheyenne Reservation. I got to know many of the people who lived there.

But each time I drove through the miles of reservation, among landscape so barren and dry that nothing could grow, I was shocked at the living conditions. Too many people lived in extreme poverty. Many of the homes were shacks with tin roofs and dirt floors. Often they had no indoor plumbing. There was no work and no way out. Stripped of self esteem and a way to make meaningful contributions to the community they loved, the Native families I knew struggled. I watched as they spent per capita checks, the blood money that the government sends to these original Americans, on old cars and alcohol. Confronted with a new awareness, I began to question a government who would strip these people of their land and banish them to a place that would keep them in poverty. I found myself embarrassed to belong to a race that had treated other human beings with such cruelty.

One afternoon I went with another volunteer to visit a family in Havre, on the Fort Belknap reservation. It was snowing and the wind was whipping across the barren, dry earth. As we pulled up to the small adobe house, a young girl came out to welcome us. She grabbed our hands and led us in. Inside, the room was full of people. A woodstove warmed the air. It was a tiny place, about 500 square feet. There were no rooms to speak of. Against the back wall, a sleeping area was marked by a tattered sheet that hung loosely from the ceiling.

We stayed there for most of the afternoon, sipping instant coffee and talking about life. There were three generations living together under one roof. I sat quietly, caught up in the energy around me, lulled by the warmth of the fire and the sound of the grandmother singing her grandson to sleep. They shared stories about their family, about life on the reservation and their dreams for their children. As we talked, the mother stood at the stove, feeding the fire and stirring a pot of venison stew. Her daughter, the girl who had come to great us, stood beside her, watching her mother drop soft doughy squares of traditional fry bread into the hot, spattering oil. As evening fell, they invited us to stay for dinner.

"Oh, no," I said. I looked at the faces around me. There were so many of them. They had so little.

"Please," she begged. "You are our guests. We want you to join us."

Although I felt guilty for accepting their invitation, we couldn't refuse. As we drove away that night, I couldn't help but reflect on what I had just witnessed. I was surprised by their kindness. Despite having everything I needed, generosity did not come easily to me. In the face of what seemed like scarcity there was abundance. I had always believed that material possessions brought happiness, but I was wrong. It was a lesson I would be reminded of again and again.

After my mother died, I found a letter I had written to her all those years ago. It was tucked in a folder filled with handwritten notes for speeches she had given over the years. It was dated October 4, 1982, just three days before her 46th birthday. I was startled to see the handwriting of a younger me, someone who could not know how she would put the pieces of a yet unfinished puzzle together. I wondered why she had saved the letter and what she had thought when she read it?

By then I was living in a trailer on the Northern Cheyenne reservation and working the night shift at a group home for Native American teens. They were troubled, having lived lives that had been ravaged by violence, substance abuse and neglect. *"The job is going OK,"* I wrote, *"Although sometimes I don't get enough sleep."* I filled her in on the things I'd been doing. *"I started an International Cooking Club with the kids and next week we will be taking them to Billings to a pro-basketball game,"* But there was also the beginning of a something deeper, words it would take me years to fully understand.

*"Tonight, one of the boys told me that the problem with these kids is that they don't believe that anyone loves them. I told them that they needed to love themselves."*

And yet, as I worked with these young victims, I began to understand that the impact I could have would be limited. Without access to the families and communities these young people would one day return to, anything we would do would never be enough. Those experiences and other like them are what led me to study family therapy and spend my career working to change the very systems that caused the problems in the first place.

As I was writing this book, I remembered the conversation I'd had with Linda, the woman my mother had supervised all those years ago and who now sat in the chair my mother had once occupied. I sent her an email, asking her if she could tell me more about my mother and the work they had done together. She sent along a booklet, created to honor the 25th Anniversary of the Somerset County Youth Services Commission, the very commission that my mother helped to establish. The booklet was filled with programs they had created over the years. "You need to know that your mother was behind every project listed," she wrote. "She is known statewide for her work in creating the blueprint for the commission. Today every county has one and most of them are fashioned on Somerset County's model."

I thought back to the comment Linda made at the funeral. *She used to gather us together in her office and tell us about what you were doing. We'd hear about the programs you were starting, about your work in Montana and on the reservation. She'd say, 'I want us to do that,' and then we'd have to figure out how.* Why hadn't I known? Why hadn't she told me she was proud of the work I was doing? "One time your mom came back from visiting you in California and said you had shared a booklet that you had created that listed all the services in your county," Linda wrote. "She was so excited about the concept that she introduced the idea to all the municipal commissions we worked with. They instituted the community Yellow Pages as a way to get out the information."

I read through Linda's email again and again. It was as if I was learning about my mother for the very first time. I had never made the connection between the path I had taken and the career my mother eventually chose but now for the first time I began to see things differently. Had my work been the catalyst for her work with the county? "She was very proud of your accomplishments as you rose to director and were teaching," Linda wrote. "She valued that you were committed to your profession as well as to your family."

My mother told others she was proud of me. I wondered why she had never done the same with me. But now, as I read the email and flipped through the pages of the book Linda sent me, I began to see something I had not seen before, a connection that had previously been invisible to me. I thought I understood the influence my mother had on me, but I had never considered the impact I had had on her.

# Chapter 13

# *Stories*

I trudged up the steps to the coffee shop and tugged at the door. Everything felt strange. Inside, the tables of the brightly lit café were filled with people. My body felt heavy as I took my place in line and waited to order my caramel latte, a treat I allowed myself when I went to the café to write.

I saw my friend Pat ahead of me and tapped her on the shoulder. "How are you?" I said. I hadn't seen her in a while.

Pat and I worked together many years ago when she was running a Youth Services Bureau for a local police department. I served as their consultant, providing family therapy supervision and training to her counseling interns. Over the time we'd worked together, we'd become friends. She was one of the most honest and true people I knew. Pat was married to a wonderful woman, a musician she'd been with for a long time.

Pat shrugged. "How are *you*?" she asked.

"I'm not good." I said as my eyes welled up with tears. I'd never been very good at hiding my feelings. Pat wrapped her arms around me and we stood there for what seemed like a long time, both of us afraid to let go.

"I know," she said. "I'm scared too. Kay and I have been crying all morning."

It was the morning of November 9th, 2016, and I could not stop crying. The night before, Donald Trump was elected president of the United States. That morning as I walked into the café and stood in line for my coffee, my brain was fuzzy and I could not feel my feet on the floor. It was as if I was in a trance. This could not be happening. It had been a long night and I'd barely slept.

The 2016 presidential campaign had been the ugliest campaign I could remember. The name calling, vitriol and misogyny had been frightening. Common decency all but disappeared. Disagreements devolved into violence. Long accepted rules of social engagement no longer stood. Racism, hatred and cruelty bubbled to the surface. Life, it seemed, had become the cruelest of reality shows, and none of us could turn it off.

Early that morning my cousin Kat sent me a text. She is the daughter of my father's middle brother. She'd seen something I'd posted on Facebook that morning. She knew I was upset. She was too. *I wonder what your father would think?* she asked.

I'd been wondering the same thing all morning. It had been more than forty years since my father first ran for office as a Republican. I had proudly campaigned for him believing with all my heart that he was an honorable man. I was hardly objective, but in Somerset County where I grew up, there were plenty of people who agreed with me.

"I think he would be horrified," I messaged back. Although my father and mother had been staunch Republicans, I believed they would have been shocked by the tenor of the recent campaign. When Richard Nixon resigned after the Watergate scandal, my father and I talked about how disappointed he was. He was disgusted with Nixon's dishonesty. It wasn't what public service was supposed to be about. Still, as my political leanings changed, I steered clear of those kinds of conversations with my parents. A few years into my social work career, I'd registered as a Democrat. After all, my life's work was about working to support the disenfranchised, to speak for people who had no voice and no representation in our system. Although we disagreed on most things political, I had a hard time believing that my father would have voted for a man like Trump.

That morning, I was overwhelmed with fear. I was frightened for the people I had spent my entire career working for. Frightened for people like Pat and my brother Robert. Frightened for the environment. For the Latino students I taught every day. I was frightened for the country and worried for my children's future.

Soon, that fear became despair. In the weeks that followed the election, my heart was heavy. I had trouble sleeping. I could not stop crying. I lost interest in doing the things of everyday life. It seemed like every conversation I had revolved around the election. I gravitated toward people who agreed with me. Who could see what I saw. As the weeks turned into months and the new administration began to unfold, I still could not regain my footing. I was glued to the television. Obsessed with the news. Sickened by every new twist and turn.

I watched as lies replaced truth. Whole groups of people insulted. Racism and violence normalized. I kept waiting for someone to make it stop. For someone to do the right thing. I kept expecting the people in power to step up the way honorable people did, but they did not. Instead they denied what we all could see. They made excuses. They pitted us against one another. The more I listened to the news, the more unbalanced I felt. It was like everything was coming unglued. With every new assault on reality I fell deeper and deeper into despair.

"Something is wrong with me," I said to my husband one night. For weeks I'd felt sick to my stomach. "I don't understand what's going on. I'm starting to wonder if something happened to me, something I don't remember." It felt like I had PTSD. I searched my memory, looking for an explanation. Had I been abused? I couldn't shake the feeling of despair, a feeling I had never felt before. I was worried. Something wasn't right. I wondered if I would ever feel normal again.

Shortly after my mother died, I'd begun to meditate. It had been difficult. Each morning I sat quietly in the living room and focused on my breath. In and out. In and out. The silence was deafening. I couldn't quiet my mind. As I tried to settle into myself, the dogs licked my hands. I thought about my mother. My children. I made lists. I'd forgotten to call the lawyer. We needed milk. I grew frustrated. I needed a focus.

I began to practice Meta, a meditation I'd learned from Sylvia Boorstein, a Buddhist teacher who I'd meant a few years before when I worked at a homeless shelter. As I felt the air in my chest rise and fall, I repeated the words she taught us. *May I be filled with lovingkindness. May I feel safe. May I feel contented, May I feel strong and may I live with ease.* It had been helpful, but now, every time I said the words *May I feel safe*, the words caught in my throat.

I kept thinking about the old children's story, *The Emperor's New Clothes*. Written by Hans Christian Anderson, it was a story about an emperor who hires a couple of weavers to make him a magnificent suit. But the weavers are conmen who know the emperor is vain, so they tell him the fabric is special, so special that it is invisible to all but the smartest in the land. His closest associates, afraid to speak up and risk falling out of the emperor's favor, play along, pretending they could see what is not there.

One day, there is a great procession through the town. As the emperor begins to march, dressed in his new invisible clothes, the townspeople line the streets and watch in uncomfortable silence. Exchanging glances, they look straight ahead, refusing to see what is right before them. Finally, a little boy in the crowd shatters the illusion. "He has no clothes," he yells. The townspeople know he is right. They can no longer pretend. They must acknowledge what they know to be true, what they have known all along. The emperor is naked.

There was something about this assault on reality that felt all too familiar. The cruelty. The lies. The abuse of power. It was all so awful. But of all of it, the worst part was the constant denial, the gaslighting of each and every painful moment. I had been that little boy, calling out to anyone that would listen. Why couldn't people see what was going on? I felt like I was going crazy.

The election opened an old wound.

Two days after my mother died, we gathered around the table at my brother's house. Father Robert, the local Catholic priest came by. He wanted to talk to us about our mother so he could prepare the homily for the funeral mass the next day.

We told him what we knew about her life in New York. We talked about the Brooklyn Dodgers, her writing career and her work in youth services. We talked about our family vacations to Lake Sebago and our trips to Europe. We pulled out family photos, black and white images of the four of us as children. We laughed as we shared childhood memories. We chose to skip over the hard stuff. You don't speak ill of the dead.

"Bea was always so supportive of me," my brother-in-law Tony said. "She encouraged me with my art. She kept pushing me to continue." In the years Robert and Tony were together, Tony began painting and had become quite successful.

My sister shot me an angry look. I nodded in agreement. It was as if he was talking about someone else.

After Father Robert left, she confronted Tony.

"I'm glad Mom was supportive to you," she said, her voice tense, "But that was not true for me."

"She was very critical of us," I said, feeling the need to explain. "Very hard on all of us. It was as if we could never do anything right."

"We were never good enough," Elisa said, adding emphasis on the word "never."

I nodded. "Remember the clothes she used to buy us?" I asked Elisa. I hated going shopping with her. While I stood in the dressing room, she brought outfit after outfit, one more ugly than the next. Things I hated. Clothes I would never have picked out for myself. I tried to resist, but she didn't care. She demanded that I try everything on. "It never mattered if we liked them."

"And she'd always buy us clothes that were too small, remember? She'd always say, 'It will fit you when you lose weight.' Can you imagine saying that to anyone?"

"And what was worse," I said. "We kept them. Why the hell did we keep them? For years I had clothes in my closet I would never wear, but I never had the courage to return them."

We all laughed an uneasy laugh. These were the things we joked about when my mother wasn't listening. The things that felt safe enough to share. But there were many more things that we never spoke about. The wounds that we carried from childhood. The struggles to connect. The loneliness we felt, even in a crowded room. We were afraid to be vulnerable with each other.

I looked around the table at my siblings, aware of both the distance between us and the ties that would always bind us. We had shared a life together that was both wonderful and painful. We had a catalogue of stories to choose from, preferring to laugh at the ones that were easier to tell. But there were others too. Painful stories that lay just beneath the surface where a scab had barely formed. Without an avenue to share them, we'd been alone in our pain. Now, our parents were gone. I wondered if we could finally be honest with each other.

It was one thing to rehash old stories, it was another to acknowledge what I knew to be true. Now that she was gone, I couldn't keep up the single family narrative, the story that we had been one big happy family. There had been many happy moments, that was true, but it was also true that there were things that happened that we needed to acknowledge. Our parents had been very hard on us. They had been abusive at times. We had had no voice. There was no room for us to speak up, to express our pain. We had been unable to speak our truth.

My mother blamed others for her anger. She was never at fault. And we were too willing to take responsibility. My father. My brothers and sister. Myself. When my mother was angry, it was always something that we had done or didn't do. We felt guilty. We apologized. We tried to make it up to her. She was a master at manipulation. Like the marionettes we played with as children, she was a puppeteer who pulled our strings.

She stirred the pot and then stood back, innocently, and waited for things to explode. She liked to be in the center of things, the hub that connected us all. She pitted Elisa against Michael. Michael against me. Our father against all of us. She played us against one another. How had she found out that I'd had sex with my boyfriend all those years ago? "Your sister read your diary," she'd said, and I'd believed her. It was only years later, when I asked my sister, that I found out it wasn't true. I wondered what else she'd lied about.

My mother was a talented storyteller. Her newspaper columns were filled with anecdotes about our family. Over the years she told many stories about the events in our lives, accounts she crafted to report, entertain and explain. These became the narratives of our life together.

One such story occurred the summer after my freshman year of college when we took a family vacation to Canada. We spent three weeks together in a borrowed 32 foot Winnebago, driving up the coast of New England to Nova Scotia and Prince Edward Island. In the fall Michael would be starting his freshman year at Stonehill College. It was a time of transition for our family.

On that trip, my father was unusually short tempered. He yelled at my mother while he maneuvered the Winnebago down the crowded island streets. After a day of sightseeing we'd pull into a campground and settled in for the night. My mother made dinner while my father mixed their nightly cocktail.

My parents were social drinkers. It wasn't unusual for them to have a Rob Roy or Martini most nights and they always drank a bottle of wine with dinner. My mother liked to joke that there was never any point in putting the cork back in the bottle. Once it was opened, it had to be finished.

But on that trip he drank more than usual. Instead of one cocktail, he would have two or three. He brooded and snapped at us over the simplest things. One night he lost it on my brother. I don't remember what Michael did to make my father so angry, I only remember feeling helpless as I stood outside the Winnebago and listened to Michael scream. After it was all over I set the table while my mother tossed the salad. We sat down to eat dinner while Michael wept. We just moved on as if nothing had happened.

As crazy as it sounds, this was not unusual. There was no discussion. No way to talk about what had occurred. No acknowledgement of what was true. It was as if it had never happened at all.

When we returned home, I asked my mother why my father had grown so angry. "He sees that the four of you have grown up," she said, "And he realizes that he missed it. He was so busy working, he wasn't around."

I felt sorry for my father. I didn't want him to have regrets. I didn't know if my mother's story was true but I accepted her explanation. It never even crossed my mind to wonder. I certainly never asked my father. But now, as I look back, I realize that in my mother's explanation, there'd been no mention of my brother. Michael had been the one who had suffered, the one who had been the victim of my father's rage. The truth was, Michael always seemed to get the worst of it. He'd been the one who'd been hurt. Not only had my mother not acknowledged it, I'd missed it as well.

As painful as it is to admit, there were other stories like this one. Times when we were overlooked, our experience ignored, our feelings discounted. Like the columns my mother wrote each week, she sold a story of our lives, a story she wanted to be true. I did not realize how willing I had been to accept her narrative, how much I had not wanted to see what was right in front of me. How blind I had been in my loyalty.

Many years ago, when I was working as a family therapist, I met a family whose son had been referred to me by his teacher at school. Sam misbehaved in the classroom, refused to do his homework and was often sent to the principal's office. At home he was defiant and disrespectful and things were getting worse. His parents had tried everything they could think of. They'd had meetings with the teachers. They'd even put him in therapy but nothing had worked. They wanted help.

Margie and Jim had an older son, Henry, who was two years older than Sam. Henry was the star of the family, a precocious straight A student who was a star athlete and well liked by everyone. The parents were at a loss. How could their two children be so different?

I invited them to come in as family and I began to draw their genogram as I had with so many families before. I asked them how they met and decided to have children.

"Henry was the perfect baby," Margie told me. "He never cried. He slept through the night almost immediately. Everyone loved him. He was always happy." Margie was very close to her mother who used to babysit Henry when Margie went to work. Shortly before she got pregnant with Sam, her mother got very sick. She was diagnosed with cancer and just before Sam was born, she died.

"I'm so sorry," I said. "That must have been very hard for your family."

"It was," she said. "I was sad for a very long time. My mother adored Henry."

But right before her mother died, Margie's mother told her something she would never forget. She told her daughter she shouldn't have a second child. That she'd never have another one as perfect as Henry.

According to Margie and Jim, her mother had been right. Sam had been trouble from the moment he was born. He'd been a colicky baby and he cried all the time. It had been hard to manage two children and the boys fought frequently. Once Sam got into school the problems got worse. It seemed like he was always in trouble. It had turned out just the way her mother predicted it would.

Except that it wasn't true. I knew it. And I think Margie knew it too. She just couldn't admit it. She couldn't betray her mother. She didn't want to be disloyal.

"Margie," I said, "Your mother was wrong. "I know how much you loved her, but Sam is every bit as perfect as Henry. You love them both."

I knew she needed to change the narrative, to confront her mother's story. I asked her to imagine telling her mother how she felt and I encouraged her to think about what she might say. A few days later, she called me to tell me that she and Jim had taken the boys to her mother's grave. "I wanted to introduce her to Sam," she told me, "It felt a little strange standing there talking into the air, but I wanted her to meet him."

For years after I stopped working with them, Margie would call me when report cards came out. Things had changed dramatically. Sam was doing great. He was more involved in school and the boys were even getting along a little better. It wasn't perfect, but it was a lot better than it had been and for that she was grateful.

I studied family therapy after years of watching the children who I'd worked so hard with revert back to old behaviors when they rejoined their family. I could no longer deny the importance of their family in their lives. I knew how important my family was to me and I thought I understood the impact they'd had, but I never imagined that working with other families would challenge me to look at my own. I'd become expert at recognizing conflicts, deconstructing the issues that caused problems in my clients' families. I challenged them to do the hard work of confronting one another, of saying the things they held back, of being really honest. It seemed so simple.

And yet, I wondered why I'd never spoken my own truth. Why I'd let my mother construct a reality that denied my own. It was one thing to do it as a child, but I'd made the same choice as an adult. Why had I continued to live by the rules we'd established long ago? Over the years I'd seen hundreds of families. Why was it I still remembered Margie's?

Perhaps it was not coincidental that once again, politics served as a catalyst to challenge me to grow. The election of Donald Trump and the death of my mother converged to reveal things I had not wanted to see, truths I had looked away from my entire life. I could no longer be clothed in denial. Like the little boy standing in the crowd, I could call out the nakedness. I could face my shame. I could finally find my voice.

# Chapter 14

# *The Contract*

A year after my mother's death I still had so many questions.

"Rob," I said as I cradled the phone between my shoulder and my ear, "Did Mom ever tell you she was proud of you?" Ever since I'd received the email from Linda, my mother's old colleague, the question had been eating away at me. Try as I might, I couldn't remember my mother ever telling me she was proud of me.

It was August of 2017. My mother had been gone for more than a year. The thick summer fog hung like a blanket over the town, mirroring my mood. No doubt, just a few miles inland, the sun had been shining all day, but days like this were common so close to the coast. I stood in the backyard and looked up at the sky, wondering if the sun would ever break through.

"She came to all of my performances," he said.

Robert is a composer. Although we'd all taken years of piano lessons, we'd been unwilling students, but as it was with most things, what my mother wanted, my mother got. We hated practicing under her critical eye. She stood over us, tapping her foot and counting aloud as she corrected our every mistake. In the end, it was Robert who gave her the musician she so desired. She nurtured his talent, making arrangements for him to travel to New York City to take private classes in composition during his high school years. Much to my parents delight, when it came time for him to go to college, he chose my father's alma mater, Yale, to study musical composition. Eventually, he earned his doctorate at the University of Pennsylvania. He now taught at West Chester University and wrote music that was performed by orchestras, symphonies and choral groups across the country. My parents rarely missed a performance.

Robert and I grew extraordinarily close in the years after my father's death as the two of us took the lead in caring for our mother. We spent hours on the phone making plans, talking through legal issues and trying to figure out how to hold things together. Sharing power of attorney, it was Robert and I who took her to Sunrise, the assisted living facility where she would eventually go to live and Robert and I who made the decisions about her care. In the six years she lived at Sunrise, I spent many weekends traveling back and forth to see her, staying at his house in the small bedroom at the top of the stairs, the bedroom his daughter affectionately called 'Aunt Suzanne's room'. We spent hours on the telephone, often speaking to each other several times a week as we navigated the final years of her life. By then, we weren't just siblings anymore. In the years caring for our mother, we'd become friends.

We still talked on the phone regularly. In the months since her death, as I struggled to make peace with my relationship with her, I had a lot of questions. I doubted my perceptions. Had things happened the way I remembered them? Had they happened at all? There were times it felt like big swathes of my memories were disappearing and the thought terrified me. My mother was in her early sixties when she'd started to forget things. I wasn't too far away from that. Could the same thing be happening to me? As I struggled to answer the questions that plagued me I often looked to Robert for answers. I counted on him to remember.

"But did she ever tell you that she was proud of you?" I asked again.

"She came to my performances," he repeated.

Robert had a tendency to always look on the bright side. As a former Eeyore, it was a quality I admired but at this moment his desire to frame my mother's behavior positively frustrated me. He was letting her off the hook. Coming to his performances wasn't the same as saying you were proud of someone. It seemed like he was making excuses for her.

"She never came to my stuff," I said. The wound still festered even all these years later.

"What did you ever do for her to come to?" he joked.

"Fuck you." I said. He could always make me laugh. "You're an asshole."

I got quiet for a moment. "But seriously, did she ever tell you that you were a good father?"

He thought for a moment. "Yes," he said. "She said we were good with Annamaria. We were together in Sanibel and Tony and I had taken them out to dinner. It must have been after you guys left. I still remember it because it was so unusual."

"Oh," I said. My heart sunk. As strange as it may sound, I always took solace in the fact that it wasn't just me. She'd never praised any of us, or at least that's what I'd thought.

"Didn't she ever say that to you?"

"No," I said.

Had she thought I was a good mother? I started to flip through my memories the way one does when they look through an old photo album. Over the years there'd been plenty of opportunities. Times when she and my father visited us in California. All those trips to Sanibel. Instead my mind settled on a time many years ago, before everything began to fall apart.

We were all in Sanibel for the annual Christmas vacation. Tucker must have been 10 or 11 at the time. He and Dylan were playing in the living room, hitting an inflated beach ball back and forth in the air. This was before my father's ALS diagnosis. Before we recognized what was happening to her. Before we knew anything was wrong. The house on Parview Drive was large and spacious. It had a kitchen that opened up to an airy great room where we often gathered in the evenings to relax, watch television and chat. The great room had a tile floor, high ceilings and tropical rattan furniture, but it was also filled with things that could break. The glass coffee tables were home to large lamps filled with seashells and my mother's collections of island pottery. Despite having six grandchildren, it wasn't really a room you'd call 'kid friendly'.

"Stop that, Tucker," I said. "You're going to break something."

I was always on guard when we visited my parents. I kept a close watch on the boys, trying to anticipate problems before they could happen. They were well behaved, for the most part, and my parents adored them, but at the same time, I could never let my guard down. I didn't want there to be any situations that would trigger their anger.

They never had much patience for mistakes. They were perfectionists and anything less was never good enough. We never argued with them. We didn't rebel. We rarely pushed back. We were all too afraid, or at least I was. I did not want to disappoint them. They demanded obedience and when we fell short, there were always consequences. They were old school. Physical punishments were common. We would line up, oldest to youngest and my mother would dole out spankings with the back of her hand, a hairbrush, a belt or whatever was handy. I wish I could say she was measured in her response, but that wouldn't be true. She took her frustrations out on us, sometimes enhancing her response by bringing in my father. "Wait 'til your father gets home," she threatened. We lived in fear of that.

It wasn't until I was much older that I realized just how good we'd been. My friends often joked about their high school years. About the time when they were suspended for skipping school. The first time they drank or snuck a cigarette. How old they were when they'd had sex for the first time. I couldn't relate to any of it. I'd been a good student. I was polite. I hadn't gotten into drugs or alcohol. We'd all gone to college. Now as I look back on it, with kids of my own, I realize all the things that could have gone wrong. We'd been pretty extraordinary, but even extraordinary had not been enough.

As much as I hated to admit it, I too had spanked my children. I'd never done what my parents did to me, but I could have. There were times when I lost control of my emotions, when my anger raged inside me, when I said things I shouldn't have. But then I was riddled with shame. How could I do what I'd promised myself I would never do? I would look at my children and see the fear in their faces and realize I had to make things right. I had to apologize. And so I did something my mother never did. I told them I was sorry. I asked for their forgiveness.

Maybe that's what underlay my hyper-vigilance when it came to Tucker's behavior that day. Maybe it was my own fear that led me to correct him. I didn't want there to be any opportunity for my parents to get angry. I didn't want my children to see what I had seen, to see their grandparents lose control. I protected them and their relationship with their Nana and Grandpa. My children loved them dearly, and I wasn't about to let that change.

The beach ball flew through the air again, this time grazing the edge of the large bamboo bookshelf that held my mother's collection of glass seashells.

"Tucker," I said, this time more sternly. "That's the second time I've had to ask you. Stop it right now." He grabbed the beach ball and put it next to him on the couch.

"Oh, leave him alone," my mother scolded. She smiled at Tucker and added a wink for good measure. "He's a good boy."

A few minutes later I went to look for her. I found her talking with Elisa in her bedroom at the back end of the house. "Can I talk to you?" I asked. I stepped into her bedroom and closed the door behind me. "Mom, please don't undermine me with Tucker."

"You're too hard on him," she said.

That was ironic coming from her.

"You don't understand." I said.

"I don't understand?" she said sharply. "I raised four children. Don't tell *me* I don't understand." She crossed her arms and turned towards me, her steely eyes locked on mine.

"Mom, please don't do this," I begged. We'd been down this road before. My mother's rage. My defensiveness. Like a movie I had seen many times before, I knew what was coming. "I don't want to do this with you again," I said. I could feel the heat rising in my cheeks. I tried to keep my composure but it was slipping away.

"Don't you dare talk to me that way," she said, squaring her body with mine. "You have no idea how much you've hurt me."

I felt my breath catch in my throat as the tears began to come. I did not move. I looked at Elisa, my eyes pleading with her for help but she stood there paralyzed. I could not think of anything to say. I was in uncharted territory. I rarely shared differing opinions with my mother. I dared not disagree with her. There was never any winning an argument with my mother. Instead they almost always occurred when she felt I'd been disrespectful. When I didn't respond in the way she wanted me to. Our relationship was a minefield. I never knew when I was in danger and the margin for error was razor thin.

This was one of those moments. I'd approached her thoughtfully, adult to adult. It never occurred to me that she would respond the way she did. Instead, her voice was sharp and caustic. Her face took on a look of condemnation I had seen so many times before. She began to recite a laundry list of failings that she had been keeping for years. *She was stunned by my disrespect. Shocked by my lack of appreciation for all that she had done for me. There was the time when I was in college that I said something cruel, something I could no longer remember. I hadn't called enough, visited enough, done enough. I didn't care about her. I didn't care about my family.* It was as if the floodgates had opened and everything came pouring out. Nothing could stop her now. She brought up things I could not recall from days I could not remember. Countless ways that I'd caused her pain.

She dove into the litany of infractions I had committed, crimes against her and my father. As her voice got louder and louder, I stood before her no longer a grown woman, a mother of two who could speak her mind. In that moment I was, again, the petulant teenager, the daughter who would never grow up. Who shamed her mother. Who did not appreciate the things that had been done for her. The daughter who, no matter what, continued to disappoint.

I would like to say that I stood up for myself, that as an accomplished woman of 42 years I held my own. I would like to say that I remained calm and clear, that I told her that she was wrong, that while I was sorry she felt the way she did, I was not responsible. I would like to say that I reminded her that all I asked was that she not contradict me in front of my child, a courtesy that she no doubt expected from her mother and everyone around her. I would like to say that I told her that I would not let her dress me down as though I was a child, that her words hurt me. After all, what could she do? She could not spank me the way she had when I was young. She could not wash my mouth out with soap for talking back. She had no power over me anymore.

But that would be a lie. I did none of the above. Instead I stood there and I listened. I sunk deeper into myself, like a turtle pulling into its shell. I returned to the child I once was, the child I always seemed to be when I was in the room with her. I did not fight back. I did not stand up for myself and although I wanted to escape, I dared not move. You did not walk out on my mother.

Not a word left my mouth. I could not say the horrible things I was thinking, the ugliness that grew in the dark places of my soul. I dared not express the feelings I had inside. *"If you can't say something nice, don't say anything at all,"* my father was fond of saying. It was a rule the children were expected to live by. Despite my parents' tendency to judge others, to say things that could hurt *us*, the message was loud and clear: *we* dare never do the same to them.

As I stood there paralyzed I wondered what she wanted from me. Did she want me to apologize? I had apologized so many times before, apologized even when I did not know what I was apologizing for. I'd simply asked for her support. I'd asked that she not interfere in my parenting. I'd asked that she respect me the way I respected her. But she could not. As she'd done so many times before, she'd turned it around and made it all about her. She'd wanted *me* to see *her*, to see the pain she was in, but it never worked the other way. She did not see me. She did not see my pain. She did not apologize. She *could* not apologize. She was never wrong.

I could not do what I had encouraged so many of my clients to do over the years. Be honest. Say what's true. Own your feelings. Be responsible for your actions. Over the years I watched it work with countless families. Through tears and heartache and difficult conversations I'd seen it transform relationships, offer families a fresh start. It required a commitment from both sides. A willingness to be vulnerable. To hear the other person. But that never happened with my mother.

By the time I left the room, I was shaking. Although we'd been through this kind of argument before, this one felt apocalyptic, like the rumbling of an earthquake that leaves a city in ruins. Each time we'd been through this in the past, I pushed through it. I let it go. I made excuses for my mother's behavior. I searched for my own responsibility. And still, I would return hoping the next time would be different.

But I was growing weary of making excuses. I was tired of taking responsibility. With each struggle I grew more angry. Each time I added another layer of emotional brickwork. It was a matter of survival. But this time felt different. The rage inside me boiled up. I felt like I might explode. I was afraid of what I might say. I clenched my jaw as I fought to control myself.

But while the aftershocks from that conversation stayed with me for a long time, below the surface something far more serious was brewing. In that moment I could not predict what was to come. I did not know that the seeds of dementia were already settling in and would soon begin erasing whole parts of her. I could not know that within a few years my father would die and leave her in our care. I did not know how our relationship would change. I could not see the devastation that was on the horizon. When she'd finished, when there was no more left for her to say, I walked back to my room, sat down on the edge of the bed and cried.

"What's the matter?" my husband asked. By then we'd been married for a long time. He'd seen these moments before. "What did she say?" he asked, but I could not answer. I shook my head slowly, as if to ease his concern. As if to say it would be OK, although I wasn't sure it would.

Soon a familiar pall settled over the house, the way it always did when my mother felt wounded. She had a way of holding us hostage as we sat for hours wondering what we'd done. I tried to pull myself together, to rejoin the rest of the group while my mother stayed in her room and smoked cigarettes, one after the other for hours.

How quickly my anger gave way to guilt. I ran through the things she'd accused me of. Had I been ungrateful? I didn't think so. Did she really believe I didn't care about her? That I didn't love my family? Nothing could be further from the truth. I'd done none of the things she'd accused me of but it hardly mattered. As they had done so many times before, her words rattled me. She was a formidable opponent and I was powerless to challenge her. She knew my Achilles heel and pointed her arrow right at it. Again, it hit its mark dead center. I felt guilty about hurting her. I felt guilty for the things I'd said. I felt guilty for not being a good enough daughter.

The dance was all too familiar. How dare I break the rules? How dare I challenge her position? It didn't matter how old I was. I didn't matter what I wanted. My needs must always be subservient to hers. I would never escape the role I had agreed to all those years ago. And perhaps, for the first time, I began to realize it would never change.

But two things can be equally true. While my head said one thing, my heart said another. Still I returned to the question that I had asked so many times before. What about the things she'd said to me? What about my hurt? *If you can't say something nice, don't say anything at all.* The rule didn't apply to her. To either one of them, actually. There'd been plenty of things she'd said over the years, plenty of times she'd hurt me. Why couldn't she ever take responsibility for her part in the problems between us? Why couldn't she see that I hurt, too? Why couldn't she say she was sorry?

A little while later my father came to find me. "Your mother is very upset," he said. "You need to go speak to her." He could not bear to see her in pain.

I opened the door to her bedroom and walked inside. She was sitting at her desk, staring out the window. The air was thick with smoke and an ashtray full of cigarette butts smoked down to the filter smoldered on the desk. I wanted to erase the past few hours. I needed to do whatever I could to relieve the tension that permeated the house. It was up to me. It was always up to me.

"Mom," I said as I stood beside her, "Please come out of your room." She had been crying. "I'm sorry," I said, my voice sounded small and weak. "I didn't mean to hurt you."

She didn't look at me. She didn't say a word. She took a long drag of the lit Benson and Hedges 100 she held in her hand and just kept staring straight ahead into space.

"I'm sorry," I said again. "Please come out of your room." After a few minutes, I turned and walked out the door.

She emerged a little while later, steering clear of me for a time. On the surface, things slowly returned to normal. I went through the motions but inside, emotions battered me like a violent storm. I was both furious and heartbroken. I felt guilty and filled with rage. I hated her and I hated myself for what I had done to her. For a while I did not bring it up with my siblings. I could not find the words to tell them what had happened. The truth was, I didn't understand it myself. Instead, someone opened another bottle of wine. The kids jumped into the swimming pool and life continued. And like so many of those moments with my mother, we just moved on. She would not acknowledge my request. She did not recognize her part. She could not own her behavior and she would not apologize. She would never apologize. And although neither of us would ever forget, we would never speak of it again.

It was a contract we made long before, one that we would never break. We were all in on it. My father, my siblings and I. We would protect her at all costs. We would not stand up for ourselves. We would not confront her. We would not speak our truth. We would never hold my mother accountable. Not ever.

I spent years trying to understand the tension between us. I ascribed my own explanation to each difficult interaction. Had she been jealous of me? She was competent and talented and brilliant beyond measure. Had we been locked in competition? She'd set the bar high. She'd wanted us to be smart, educated and successful and yet she could never give us credit. We had all done good things. Gone to college. Had careers. Families. She'd wanted our light to shine, but not too brightly. She was never very good at sharing the spotlight.

I wondered if my siblings felt the ache I did. I wondered if they'd also wanted the connection with her that I so desperately sought. Perhaps Elisa. Yes, Elisa. She too wanted my mother to see her. But my brothers? Did my brothers want the same thing I'd wanted? The responsibility of being her daughter hung heavy on me. I'd tried hard to make her proud. I did everything she'd asked me to do. Why then did I feel like it hadn't been enough? Like I was never enough. Why did I still care?

After my mother died I called her brother. Over the years he'd been the one I went to when things got difficult with my mother, when I needed someone to talk to. I told him things I could never say to her. I wanted him to listen, to validate my thoughts and feelings and he'd been a good ally. But now that she was gone, I was filled with questions. I hoped he could answer them.

"What was it like to grow up with her?" I asked. Like me, my mother was the oldest in her family too. My uncle Vic was three years younger. Their sister Annamaria, three years younger still.

"You mother was a star," he said. "She was always the center of attention." He told me stories of watching her perform, times when the whole family became her audience.

"But what about you and Auntie Re? What was your relationship like with her?" I asked.

"I'm not sure she even noticed us," my uncle had said. "It was as if Annamaria and I didn't exist."

She'd grown up believing that she was the only one that mattered. As if the rest of the family had just been supporting actors whose only purpose was to enhance her performance. When the curtain came down, she'd never turned to thank the cast who stood beside her. She'd never even noticed that they were there. I wondered why my grandparents hadn't intervened. Why they'd let her get away with it. But the truth was, I had done the same thing. We all had.

I spent my whole life waiting for her to notice me. I learned my lines well. I acted my part. I strove to make her proud and waited to be recognized. I waited for the applause that would never come. And still I kept hoping.

But I too had been complicit. I too stood silently as over and over again she took center stage. I stood in the shadows afraid to speak the lines I'd spent all those years rehearsing. I'd been afraid to show myself, afraid to claim my spot, afraid to change the script. Although she could not see the character I had become, I never gave up hope. Instead of speaking, I chose to stay silent, waiting for a moment that would never come. But now, as I looked back at our lives together, I couldn't help wondering what might have happened if I had chosen differently. If I had seen things more clearly. Would it have made a difference? And to whom?

# Chapter 15

# *Maman*

In the summer of 2012, I applied for Italian citizenship. The Italian Embassy was at the top of a hill on Divisidero Street, in an elegant old white Victorian. As I drove through the hilly San Francisco neighborhood, I caught sight of the familiar red, white and green flag as it flapped in the gentle breeze. I found a parking spot just around the corner and pulled my light blue CRV alongside the curb. My stomach was in knots with excitement. I had been waiting for this day for a very long time.

I rang the doorbell and waited to be buzzed in.

"Buongiorno," came the voice through the small speaker on the wall. "Can I help you?"

"I have an appointment for citizenship," I said.

"Name?"

"*Mah-jeo.*" I said, using the Italian pronunciation. In Italian "Maggio" meant the month of May.

"Buongiorno, Senora Maggio" the gentleman said as I stepped up to the counter. "Do you have your documents?" I handed him the folder filled with papers I'd been collecting for months. "Please have a seat," he said after he flipped through them. "Someone will be with you in a few minutes."

I found an empty seat in the row of folding chairs along the wall. There were a few other people already there. I made eye contact with the young woman who sat across from me and smiled a half smile. *A student, I guessed, perhaps here to get a visa for her study abroad program.* A phone rang and I listened as the man I had just spoken to addressed the caller in Italian. I smiled to myself. I was really here.

The building was old but well appointed with high ceilings and hardwood floors. The walls were filled with black and white pictures of familiar scenes in Italy. The Piazza San Marco in Venice. The Roman Coliseum. A street scene in Naples. Each reminded me of the pencil and ink drawings I'd received from my aunts in Rome when Bob and I got married. They hung in the hallway of our house, a constant reminder of my family far away. The minutes ticked by. Each time the door opened I felt my heart flutter, hoping it would be for me. Finally, after waiting for what seemed an eternity, I heard someone call my name.

The neatly dressed woman who met me at the door had dark hair and polished red nails and reminded me of Lauretta, my mother's cousin in Rome. Once inside, I was surprised at how big the office was. The large room was filled with desks and cubicles and at least a dozen or more people.

"Documenti?" the consul asked when I was seated in his office. For months I had been collecting dozens of documents, sending requests to gather birth certificates for my father and mother, myself and both sets of grandparents. Marriage certificates and death certificates. My grandfather's naturalization papers. I had written to my cousin Paola to ask if she could help me get my grandfather's birth certificate from the office in Rome. She'd sent her father, my mother's first cousin, to collect it for me. It had arrived a month before, special delivery, from Italy. All of the documents had to be original. All had to be certified and translated into Italian.

"Why do you want citizenship in Italy?" the consul asked.

I swallowed hard as I felt the words catch in my throat. "My grandfather was from Rome," I heard myself say and I could feel my eyes well up with tears. It was such a simple response. The truth was so much more complicated than that.

From the time I first skipped rope with my cousins on Via Giacomo della Porta, I longed to be Italian. It was something I felt deep inside. Something I could not explain. By the time I sat in front of the Italian consul, it had been more than 30 years since I'd been back. In those years I'd married, built a career and raised two children. When I'd gotten married I'd struggled with changing my name. My husband's family was Bohemian and I did not want to leave my Italian heritage behind. But as I look back, I realize it was more than that. I felt like I was losing something, something I wanted desperately to hold on to. My name was my identity. I could not give up the connection to my family. In the end I hyphenated my name and created an unpronounceable mouthful not only for me but for our children. Despite its legal standing, it is a name my children and I rarely use.

In the thirty years since I'd been back to my beloved Italy I'd immersed myself in family life, in making school lunches and attending parent teacher conferences, sewing Halloween costumes and overseeing school projects. Engrossed in my life in California and far away from the family I had grown up in, I began to feel farther and farther removed from the Italian traditions that had once meant so much to me. And, as my mother continued to slip away, I began to feel like a part of me was slipping away too.

The consul took a pen and drew a line though the hyphenated surname I'd written on the form. "Your name is Maggio," the consul said, correcting the form. "We don't use the married name." I breathed a sigh of relief as though his words validated what I knew in my heart. *I was born a Maggio. I would always be a Maggio.*

As I drove home that day over the Golden Gate Bridge, I was filled with excitement and anticipation. I felt like Pinocchio, the little wooden boy who longed to be real. Although the choices I'd made took my life in a different direction, far away from the complicated family I loved, I never let go of the connection to my family heritage. It was one of the things I had always been most proud of. Now, no one could take it away from me. One day soon, I would really be Italian.

I longed to go back to Italy, but for years it had been beyond reach. There always seemed to be more bills than money and my commitment to my responsibilities overshadowed my dreams but in the fall of 2011 something unexpected happened. In the years after I closed the Family Institute of Marin, I began teaching Psychology at a local college. One afternoon, as I was walking across campus on my way to class, I saw a poster for the school's study abroad program. The college was recruiting instructors to teach in Florence and Barcelona.

I stood and stared at the poster, my heart racing with anticipation and in that moment I was sure about one thing. I had to go. I submitted my application and shortly thereafter was granted an interview. By then Tucker was in his sophomore year at Cornell and Dylan, his senior year in high school. Soon Bob and I would be empty nesters and every time I thought of it, the idea terrified me. For 20 years I'd thrown myself whole-heartedly into motherhood and I'd loved every minute of it. The noisy family meals and the elementary school talent shows. There were middle school band concerts and more high school football games than I could count. I remembered making small adobe bricks for the fourth grade mission report and dozens of pink and white frosted cookies each Valentine's Day. But now, as Dylan's senior year ticked by and the prospect of an empty nest grew more real, I wondered who I would be if I wasn't a mother. I'd given everything to my children. As I thought about Dylan leaving, I felt a part of me being ripped away and I wondered what, if anything, would be left.

"You've applied to go to Florence," the department chair said, "Would you be open to Barcelona?"

"Yes," I said, not wanting to jeopardize my chances. Although I had my heart set on Florence, I really would go anywhere they would send me. A few days later I was accepted. In the fall of 2012, I would be on my way to Barcelona.

I spent months getting ready. There was so much planning to do. I took a leave of absence from the homeless shelter where I'd been working as the clinical director in addition to my teaching duties at the college. I had curriculum to write. Meetings to attend. It was as if I was pushing pause on the life I was living and walking into something new, something I could only imagine. While Dylan attended his senior prom, played in his final baseball game and completed his senior project, I bought plane tickets and applied for a Spanish visa. I rented a little place to live in the Eixample section of Barcelona, a furnished, two-bedroom apartment that belonged to a Spanish artist who was living in Michigan. For the first time in my life, I'd be living alone. I was both nervous and excited as hell. I couldn't wait to leave.

In Barcelona, I signed up for a week of Spanish classes at a local language school. I'd taken 6 years of Spanish in junior high and high school. While it had been a while, I was sure that with a little work it would all come back. I planned for Bob and the boys to meet me when the semester was over. I'd take them to Italy to visit some of the places I'd loved as a child. We'd go to Florence, Venice and they'd meet their cousins in Rome. I couldn't wait to show them all the things that had meant so much to me.

By then my mother had been living at Sunrise, the assisted living facility, for almost two years and in that time we'd developed a routine. Every three months when I'd go to visit, my brother and I would drive along the Delaware River to Yardley, Pennsylvania and stop at McCaffrey's, a local grocery store, to pick up a pastry. My mother, who'd always worried about her figure, now ate pecan ice cream and rich sugary donuts. We'd pull into the parking lot of the big yellow colonial, enter the code to the locked door in the back wing and let ourselves in. Many times, my mother would be waiting for us, seated in an overstuffed chair and dressed in clothes we could not identify, clothes that did not belong to her. Sometimes she would recognize us. More often, she did not.

Her face began to change. Her skin, once taught and tanned, hung off her cheekbones and gathered in folds around her neck. Her thick hair was often unkempt and the women who cared for her dressed her in sweatshirts she would never have been caught dead in. She'd always been someone who was deeply concerned about the way she looked. I couldn't help feeling that she would be horrified if she could see herself now. As the months passed and she continued to slip away, I searched for things about her I still recognized, afraid that soon the mother I knew would be gone forever. But something else began to eat away at me. With each visit I couldn't shake the feeling that my own identity was being threatened too, that somehow losing her meant losing a piece of myself as well.

With each visit I felt increased sadness as I realized that any hope of a real relationship with her was gone. Perhaps I already knew. Ever since that day in Sanibel when we'd had that horrible argument, something inside had shifted. It was as if a part of me had given up, let go of the hope that things would ever be different, and yet? There were so many things we had in common, so many things I had wanted to share but over the years it was the differences that I clung to, that I wanted others to see. "I am *not* my mother," I said again and again. "I am *not* my mother." Now, as she slowly slipped away, I wondered what was left. If I wasn't her, who was I?

A month before I left for Spain, I went to say goodbye. It was a muggy day in late July. Robert and I signed our names on the guest log, punched in the code on the keypad and entered through the locked door. Just past the nurse's station, the staff set the tables for lunch. My mother was waiting for us, sitting with one of the other residents in front of the television in the day room.

"Your family is here, Bea," Tasheba announced loudly. Her confident voice boomed through the room. The director of the facility, she was the one I called when I needed things done for my mother. I'd spoken to her on the telephone many times over the past few years, but this was the first time I'd actually met her in person. Like many of the staff at Sunrise, she adored my mother.

"Hi Mom," Robert and I said in unison. We leaned in and gave her a kiss on opposite cheeks.

"Do you want to go out for a while?" Robert asked, not waiting for an answer. I helped her up from the couch and began to walk with her towards the door. I wanted to get out of there. It was a nice facility, bright and airy and the staff tried their best to make it feel like a home, but I was never comfortable there. The sight of men and women sleeping in their wheelchairs while others aimlessly wandered the halls broke my heart. They all seemed so fragile and disconnected. I did not want to accept that my mother was like them, or that they were like her. Someone's mother, father, sister or brother. In all the years that she lived at Sunrise, I never got used to seeing her there.

She spoke less and less these days and when we visited, our conversations fell into a familiar pattern. We bantered back and forth between ourselves, as if she wasn't there. When we did speak to her we spoke loudly and slowly, like we were talking to a child. We'd even taken to answering our own questions. With our mother in the back seat, Robert and I chatted away while we drove to the cafe down the street and ordered her a roast beef sandwich, rare, just the way she liked it.

"I'm going away for a while," I said as I sat beside her. It would be many months before I would get back to see her again. I pushed away the thought that this might be the last time I would *ever* see her. "I'm going to teach in Spain."

She looked at me as I spoke but I wondered if she understood what I was saying. "In Barcelona," I continued. "I'm going to Barcelona." I paused for a moment the way you do when you expect the other person to say something. When you wait for some feedback to come your way. She had always been someone who was not afraid to share an opinion or give advice whether you wanted it or not, but nothing came.

"Remember all the times we went to Europe?" I continued, filling the awkward silence after I realized I was waiting for a response that would never come. "Remember when we went to Spain? I'm going back. I'm going to go back to all the places you took us to and I'm going to see them again."

In the months ahead I would be retracing the steps we had taken together so many years before and forging new paths as well. If only I could ask her questions about the places we'd gone as children. If only she could help me plan. She'd always been so good at that. Funny how I'd never really appreciated the way she'd planned each day to the minute. I'd become annoyed when she quizzed us on all of it afterwards. I'd never wanted her advice before, but now, when I needed her most, she was barely there.

"I'm going to go Rome," I said. "I'm going to see our family. Elisabetta, Paula and Zio Dino." I wanted her to see how excited I was.

"Do you remember the night in the Piazza Navona?" I asked. I remembered it like it was yesterday. Running around the square with my cousins. The sound of water splashing from Bernini's fountain. The taste of the chocolate tartuffo from Tre Scalini. As we often did when we visited her, Robert and I filled the spaces for her. We laughed as we shared the memories from long ago.

My mother smiled as her eyes met mine. "Maybe," she said and then she paused for a moment. Her voice sounded so small and innocent, like the voice of a child. "Maybe I could come and visit you."

She *had* been listening. I looked into her eyes and forced a smile, my heart breaking as the words came out of my mouth. "Maybe you could, Mom," I said. "Maybe you could."

A month later we moved Dylan into Catherine and Mary, his dorm at Gonzaga University, a small Jesuit college in eastern Washington. All day I had been fighting the temptation to dissolve into a pool of tears. Here I was, a month after leaving my mother, saying goodbye to another piece of me. Dylan and I had gotten so close the past year, I was really going to miss him. Now, as Bob and I were preparing to leave, I was fighting hard to hold it together. I folded and refolded the clothes in his dresser. Organized his desk and loaded the paper in his printer, delaying the inevitable as long as I could.

"It's time to go," my husband said dispassionately.

*I know,* I thought. I didn't need him to say it. I held Dylan tight as we said goodbye, the tears streaming down my face.

"I'm probably not going to miss you," I whispered, attempting a joke.

"Me neither," he said. I did not want to let go. I hugged him one more time and then watched as he walked back into the dorm, turning to wave goodbye. I climbed into the rental car and stared out the window trying hard to compose myself. An hour later as I sat on the plane, I watched as the last few bags were loaded into the cargo hold. My heart ached. My thoughts were filled with images of the past eighteen years. Tears flowed down my cheeks. How had the time gone so fast?

"It seems like a great place," my husband said.

"Yeah," I said, barely turning to look at him. I wasn't up for talking. Bob had been surprisingly supportive of my plan to teach abroad and I was grateful for that. As the plane taxied down the runway, my thoughts turned to what was to come. In five days I would be boarding a plane bound for Spain. I couldn't wait to leave.

A week later I stepped out of the taxicab in front of an apartment building on a Barcelona street, the Carrer de Diputacío, #73. I was tired and hungry but so excited I could barely contain myself. I collected the keys to the apartment and took the elevator to the fourth floor. The apartment was stark, not at all what I had expected. The walls were white, the ceiling high. I pushed my bags into the corner of the entryway and head down the hall. There was a bedroom to the right and across the narrow hall, an office. The bathroom was tiny. You could wash your face, use the toilet and take a shower without moving more than a foot. There was a second bedroom and a small kitchen. Straight ahead, through two narrow stained glass doors, were two more rooms, a dining and living room, with tall wooden shutters that opened out onto the street.

The apartment was modestly furnished. A tall, dark, antique oak buffet with a big rectangular mirror. An old wooden table and four chairs. A tiny side table with a telephone and answering machine. A small, off-white modern sofa that doubled as a bed. A small armoire, a television and a light wood coffee table.

I rolled my suitcase down the hall to the bedroom. My bedroom. I lifted it up, placed it on the bed and began to unpack. Before I left for Barcelona, my friend Lesley took me shopping for new clothes. "You can't dress like that in Spain," she'd said to me, smiling as she looked disapprovingly at my well-worn capris and oversized men's shirts. I had always hated shopping, but I couldn't turn Lesley down. We went to her favorite little boutique and, as I stood helpless in my underwear and bra, she passed one outfit after another over the dressing room door. I smiled to myself as I hung up the new clothes. I paired my shoes and lay them neatly in a row at the bottom of the closet. Despite the weight of my suitcase, there wasn't much there.

I placed my laptop on the desk in the office and fished through my suitcase for the power strip I'd brought from home. I plugged it into an adapter and flipped the switch. There was a pop. A puff of smoke. The strong smell of something burning. And then, darkness.

Shit.

I realized right away what I had done. I felt my way down the wall until I found the outlet. I unplugged the power strip, hoping that that would solve the problem. It did not. Feeling around in the dark, I worked my way down the hallway, using the walls to guide me. I opened the shutters to the street, expecting to illuminate the room, but all I saw was darkness. My heart pounded in my chest as I ran my hand across the table, fishing for my cell phone. Outside, the sound of the traffic filled the air. Spanish voices rose up from the cafe below. I wondered if anyone could help me but I didn't know how to ask. My heart was racing. I was on my own.

I fumbled with the telephone, trying to call home hoping Bob could help but I couldn't figure out how to make an international call. At some point I thought to search for the fuse box. I pressed the buttons on my iPhone and used the light to navigate my way down the hall. I walked in and out of the rooms, searching for anything that looked familiar. Nothing. After a few minutes I noticed a small sliver of light under the door coming from the foyer. I rushed to the door and yanked it open. Light filled the hallway. There, to the right of the doorway was the fuse box. I threw open the door and flipped the breaker.

A few minutes later, I looked down at the street and watched for a while as people wandered up and down the sidewalk. At street level, the white cloth covered tables of the Cafe Mediterrani were full of people. My stomach was growling. For months I'd imagined myself sitting with a glass of Rioja and a big plate of paella, chatting away in flawless Spanish. My mouth watered as I tasted the imaginary forkful of seafood infused rice and sipped the fruity red wine. But that would have to wait for another day. I'd barely managed enough Spanish to give the address to the cab driver and as hungry as I was, I couldn't quite muster enough courage to head downstairs. Tomorrow would be different, I told myself. Tomorrow *I* would be different.

At the airport I'd bought a package of trail mix and a small bottle of lemonade from a vending machine. I still had the lemonade. The trail mix was stale, but there was still half the bag left. That would have to do. I checked the tiny freezer for ice cubes, but there were none. Grabbing a glass from the kitchen, I filled it with warm lemonade. I sat down at the dining room table and ate my first meal in Barcelona.

Laughter rose from the cafe below. Motor scooters buzzed down the street. Next door, I heard my neighbors chattering away, banging pots and pans as they made dinner. I was exhausted. I left the dirty glass and the wrapper from the trail mix on the dining room table and walked down the hall to the bedroom. It had been a long day. I pulled off my clothes and dropped them on the floor at the foot of the bed. I put on my nightgown and climbed beneath the crisp white sheets. I stared up and the ceiling and smiled in the darkness. I wanted to pinch myself. I was finally here.

A month later, my friend Diane, a fellow teacher and I walked along the banks of the Nervión, a river in Bilbao, Spain. After that first night, things had settled down. The week of Spanish classes had been helpful, but I was far from conversant. I mixed up verbs and tenses and the few Italian words I knew crept into my Spanish conversations. When I wasn't teaching, I spent my free time wandering the neighborhoods. The Barri Gotic. The Raval. Gracia, Barcelonetta and my neighborhood, Le Eixample. I looked forward to the walk to school and the chance to stop and pick up fruit or bread at the local market. I spent hours snapping pictures, breathing in the smells of this magnificent city. I was happier than I had been in months.

The sunlight sparkled on the shimmering walls of the Guggenheim museum. Maman, the enormous metal spider sculpture by Louise Bourgeois was cloaked in fog, a sculpture by the Japanese artist Fujiko Nakaya. The spider towered over us. A sack of glass eggs hung below her body. Maman was the French word for mother. As I walked by, I couldn't help but think of my mother, so far away. She had studied French in college. Like me, she preferred the classics. I thought back to the first time she took us to St. Peter's Basilica to see Michelangelo's Pietá. I wondered what she would think of Bourgeois' modern tribute to her own mother who was also her best friend.

The Guggenheim was our first stop in Bilbao. Diane, an artist who taught Art History and drawing, loved modern art and the Guggenheim was filled with some wonderful works. We planned to visit the museum and then ride the train to San Sebastian. I, on the other hand, had always preferred the more traditional works of the Italian Renaissance, the dark brooding of the Dutch masters or even the more romantic scenes of the French impressionists. These were the works I'd seen when I'd traveled to Europe as a child. The paintings of Botticelli and da Vinci. The sculptures of Rodin and Bernini. It seemed like such a long time ago that I'd taken all those courses in Art History and planned to earn a Master's degree in Fine Arts. At the time I knew how to discuss the use of religious symbolism, the interplay of light and shadow and to articulate the artist's intention, but modern art had always confused me. Although I'd been exposed to the works of Miró and Modigliani, Dali and Kandinsky, I had to confess I couldn't make much sense of it.

The Guggenheim building was a work of art in itself. I was mesmerized by the way Frank Gehry, the architect, played with shape and space and material. As we walked towards the entrance, a bride and groom strolled up the steps, stopping to pose for photographs. I fished in my pocket and pulled out a few Euros to pay my admission. I tuned in the audio guide, hoping it might help me understand what I was about to see.

On the first floor, Richard Serra's large, bronze steel sculpture, The Matter of Time, filled the room. As I walked through the tall, fourteen-foot series of spirals, ellipses and circles, I felt dizzy, disoriented and confused. I had been taught to understand art through the medium of language. To explain what the artist was trying to achieve through their work. Recognizable images did that for me. Botticelli's Venus emerging from a scallop shell. Monet's Garden at Giverny. Even Van Gogh's Starry Night was easier to comprehend. But this was different. This was visceral. As I made my way through the exhibit, I was at a loss to explain what was going on.

"Just experience it," Diane said over and over.

And so I wandered from room to room, fighting the need for an explanation, something that might help me understand. Instead, I allowed myself to just be in it. Phrases in English, Spanish and Catalan moved horizontally in blue LED lights across a red backdrop. This work was created to bring attention to the AIDS epidemic. I thought of my friends who had died over the years and those who were still living with the disease. In another room, a wooden sculpture of screens, entitled Jealousy, made me think of Catholic confessionals. Was that what the artist intended? I challenged myself just to notice what I was feeling rather than always trying to understand.

My shoes squeaked on the hardwood floor as I stepped into a room filled with 5 by 7 black and white photographs of faces. They covered the walls from floor to ceiling: young and old, men and women, victims and criminals, students, parents, children. From the ceiling hung a series of single incandescent light bulbs, their soft yellow glow filling the room.

I stepped into the center. Surround by dangling lights, my eyes locked onto the eyes in the photographs. As I looked at the images that surrounded me, I swallowed hard and then, without warning, I began to cry.

"In your face are the faces of those who have come before," I heard the artist Christian Boltanski say as I listened through the headphones.

My father. Grandpa Basili. My maternal great grand-mother, Nonna, and Grandma Gulotta. My mother. My own Maman. They were with me. They would always be with me.

# Chapter 16

# *The Ties That Bind*

Ten months after my mother died, Michael's only daughter got married. Although I'd tried to move on from the disappointment I'd felt in his absence from our lives, I still had hurt feelings lingering just below the surface. As with every other conflict in our family, we never really spoke about what had happened. For a time I wondered if he would invite me to the wedding. For nine years we'd been bound together by the promise we'd made to our father, but now that our mother was gone, there was no imperative to stay together, no contract to uphold. When the wedding invitation came in the mail, there was never any question if I would go. He wanted me to be there and despite the struggles we had been through, I wanted to be there too.

The autumn sun hung low in the sky and cast a golden glow on the cottages that lined the shore. The New England fall colors washed the leaves of the trees in beautiful reds, yellows and shades of orange. The tiny lakeside chapel was just beginning to fill. A stream of family and friends took their seats, some I knew and many I did not.

I greeted my brother outside the chapel. It had been quite a year. Ten months earlier we'd gathered on a snowy hillside in Lambertville to put my mother to rest. A few months later, we'd emptied out the storage unit.

It was all that was left, the stuff we thought we might want someday. One by one we pulled out the boxes and put them down in the parking lot. The cold March wind whipped through our coats. I pushed a set of keys against the packing tape and tore open a box. None of us had thought to bring a knife. Dozens of green packing peanuts flew into the air.

"Oh my god, remember these?" Elisa said as she carefully opened a bubble wrapped package. A hand carved character, a man dressed in colorful lederhosen and a matching hat, sat atop a wooden napkin ring. My parents bought them on a trip we had taken to Germany when I was 12 years old. There had been six of them, one for each of us, but Elisa could only find three. The moveable head of the man was a bit wobbly. The elastic had lost its tightness over the years and one of the rings had cracked, but it was nothing that a little bit of glue couldn't fix.

I slit open another box and dug through the foam peanuts. Inside was a beautiful Deruta platter with a traditional Raffaellesco dragon painted in yellows, blues and seafoam green. Like my mother, I loved Italian pottery. Over the years of travel with my father she had amassed a large collection of pieces. While they were all beautiful, there were a few of them that held special memories. A red rooster pitcher that she bought in a small shop in Sienna. A set of three dishes handpainted in different colors that had hung on the wall in the house on Preston Drive and a set of four red and white demitasse cups. As a child it was my chore to make the espresso, filling the metal Mocha pot with water and Medaglia D'Oro grounds and placing it on the stove until the water pushed its way to the top.

There was a beautiful plaque of The Canticle of the Creatures that she bought in Assisi. My mother loved St. Francis, and the set of hand painted tiles hung on the walls of all of the houses at one time or another; on the porch on Preston Drive, in the sunroom at the house at Lake Valhalla and on the patio at Sanibel.

"I think I found Dad's golf clubs." Michael's voice jolted me out of my memories. There were four long boxes tucked in the back of the unit. "I'd like a set of these... if that's OK with everybody else."

"Of course," I said. None of the rest of us played golf. When my kids were little, my parents taught them how to swing a club, taking them out on the 6th hole in the late afternoon, after the serious golfers were finished. My father even cut down a putter for each of the boys so they could have their own club to practice with. I would take a set of clubs for each of them.

But besides the pottery, there were only two things that I wanted; my mother's notebooks and one of my father's ship models.

After he retired, my father began building model ships. They were remarkable structures with tiny match-sized gangplanks and tightly knotted rigging. Hand cut white canvas sails were attached to the masts and rowboats with tiny oars hung from the hull. Both Robert and Elisa already had one and ever since his death in 2007, I'd wanted one too. The first one he ever built had always been my favorite. It had big billowy sails and a hull covered in tiny pieces of copper that he glued by hand. That was the one I wanted.

Inside the storage unit were two ships, the one with the copper encased hull and a schooner that I didn't remember, built without sails but with a remarkable mass of intricate rigging. While the schooner remained intact, the protective Lucite case of the copper hulled ship had collapsed and snapped the mast in two. Moisture from a leak in the storage unit caused the pristine white sails to mold and the copper hull, now missing some of the tiles, had tarnished with age. My heart sank. The ship was ruined.

Michael took the schooner. I began to search for the notebooks. I found them tucked in a blue plastic box, along with reams of my mother's writing.

By late in the afternoon, we'd divided up what was left. In addition to the golf clubs and the ship model, Michael took a painting my parents bought in a gallery in Kennebunkport one summer when we vacationed in Maine. Elisa took home the antique lions head table where we had shared so many meals over the years. And Robert, a set of beautiful dishes and a carved wood wall hanging of the Last Supper. As we sorted through the boxes we talked back and forth, telling various stories we remembered. We would all go home with something, these remnants of our life together. One day we might give them to our children.

I shipped the box of my mother's writing back to California. It would be many months before I would open it. Inside there were large scrapbooks filled with clippings of her newspaper columns. Hundreds of them it seemed. There was a collection of letters from my father, letters he'd written to her before they were married during his first year at Yale. And there were a dozen or so manuscripts, many I had never seen before, stories she'd written over the years and letters from publishers she had solicited, rejections every one.

I rifled through the box until I found one I did remember, *Luigi's Shirt*. It was the story of Luigi Beccalli, a friend of my grandfather's from Italy. Luigi was an athlete, a world-class runner that represented Italy in the 1932 and '36 Olympics. My mother adored Luigi, and every year when her family went to their summer house in High Bridge, Luigi would come to visit. According to the story, he taught my mother to play the Italian card games, tre sette and scoppa. On warm summer days they would walk into town along the long country road to get ice cream. And when Luigi and my mother held races on the bocce court, he always let my mother win.

One day, back in Brooklyn, when she and her siblings were playing in their basement, they found a shirt in an old steamer trunk. Although it was yellowed with age, the sleeveless white knit had a green and red stripe and an emblem encircled in gold braid. It was Luigi's Shirt, her father told her, the shirt that he wore when he won the gold medal in the 1500-meter race in the 1932 Olympics in Los Angeles. He had given it to my grandfather as a gift of their friendship.

Luigi's jersey hung in my mother's office, framed with a newspaper clipping from the New York Times, *"Beccalli of Italy Wins 1500 Meters at Olympic Games."* After we sold the house in Montville, it ended up in my brother's basement. I discovered it one weekend when I'd gone to visit.

"What's Luigi's shirt?" my brother asked when I showed him. Evidently she'd never told him the story.

We'd shared my mother's columns at her funeral. "Nana wrote like you," Tucker said when he and Dylan sat huddled together on the couch, the big brown binder spread across their laps. "Did Uncle Michael really lose his turtle in the house?"

"Yes," I said. "The turtle's name was Uncle Vic, named after Nana's brother. We found him crawling under the piano."

"I can actually hear you saying this," Dylan said. "Nana was a good writer."

"She was," I said, but even as the words left my mouth, I wondered if I'd ever told her. The truth was, I wrote like her, not the other way around.

In the years since her death, I've sorted the memories of what was from the wishes of what would never be. My parents had asked me to make an impossible choice, one no daughter should ever have to make. My family or myself. To choose one meant to let go of the other and so, for much of my life, I felt suspended between the two. I could not choose.

But now I know it was a false choice. It wasn't either/or, it was both/and. In the years since her death I have come to understand that I can have both. I can be both. I am both a part of the Cardinal Club and separate from it. I am different from my mother and I am the same. Both parts live in me.

My brother looked handsome in his dark grey suit, smiling as he said hello. I wrapped my arms around him and gave him a hug, kissing him on the cheek. He was thinner, more at peace than he'd been in a while. He'd recently started a new job and he was hopeful for what was to come. I took my seat in the chapel and looked out at the lake. I had been thinking about my mother since I'd woken that morning. That day would have been her 80th birthday.

My nephew walked his mother down the aisle. I couldn't remember how long it had been since I had last seen him. Only one of Michael's children came to my mother's funeral. Back when we gathered at the house in Sanibel, the kids would spend days on the beach building sand castles and jumping waves together. But now their lives had taken them in different directions. It had been years since they slid down the nautilus slide at the Sun Dial resort or talked to the big brightly colored parrots at Jerry's market. It seemed so long ago. Did they have anything in common anymore?

And yet, that night I watched as my kids talked to their cousins. They huddled together, their grown bodies dressed in suits and ties, held together by an invisible bond. They were no longer the children they once were. Now they lived in the same cities. Worked long hours trying to find their way in the world. Maybe they could get together for dinner or drinks? "We're going to have you over," my niece told my youngest. I hoped they would.

As we sat together under the moonlit sky, my sister began to tell me about a project she was working on. Over the past few years she'd been using art as a therapeutic medium. She'd put together a book of pieces she'd created and was thinking about offering healing workshops locally, teaching people the therapeutic process that she'd found so helpful. I was glad that she'd found something that made her happy. As I listened to her, my mother's words rang in my ears. *Family is the most important thing you will ever have. Friends may come and go, but family is forever.*

The evening was beautiful. We ate and danced and laughed together. As my nephews toasted their sister, their love for her was palpable. Michael was a good father. I wished my father could have been there to see his oldest son. I knew he would be proud. I wished our parents could be there to see the family that they had created. We were all there. Though the road had been a rough one, we had found our way back.

I put my arms around my brother at the end of the night. "Thank you for including us in this celebration." I said. I choked out the words through my tears. I'd been hanging on to hurt feelings for so long. It was time to let them go.

"Thank you," he said. "Thank you for coming all this way to celebrate with us. I know it wasn't easy. It means a lot."

After my mother died I began to feel a responsibility I was just beginning to understand. I had taken my family for granted, believed that they would always be there. But now as I hugged my brother goodbye, I understood things differently. Like my father's collection of ship models, there were new boats in the harbor. As our children married and formed their own families, it was our turn now. Family was a choice, a choice that belonged to each of us. Now that my mother and father were no longer there to hold us together it was up to us to decide what we wanted to be to each other, if we would move forward, and how.

I, for one, was clear. I would do all I could to help us find our way back to each other because like my mother, I too believed that family was forever.

# *Epilogue*

Dark clouds hovered above, threatening rain. I peeked out from under the canvas that covered the sides of the large transport truck that took us up the mountain and looked up at the Nicaraguan sky. Just a few hours before, when we were still at the worksite, the sun's rays scorched our skin. But this was summer in the mountains. I gripped the steel bars as we bounced along and listened to some of the teenagers, Hannah, Cece and Bea, sing show tunes.

"That's my mother's name," I'd said to Bea when I met her. I noticed that I used the present tense. I didn't tell her that my mother was dead. I paused for a moment to consider the coincidental timing. Funny how I'd never met anyone named Bea before.

As the truck winded its way out of town, we turned right, up a rough dirt road. At the intersection, the truck paused for a moment as a woman and her son climbed into the back with us, but soon we were on our way again, bumping along. Voices filled the air. It was hard to believe that just a few days before, when we huddled together at the airport, we hardly knew each other's names.

For several years I have been bringing students to rural communities in Nicaragua to build schools and learning centers with the hope of improving the education system for the children of this Central American country. We dig ditches, mix cement and build walls and we learn about a life very different from our own. "Turn off your cell phones," I always tell the students when we get ready to board the plane. "I want you to look around. Slow down. Pay attention. Be present."

It's been more than a year since my mother died. I thought about her every time I traveled and this time is no different. As I hand my passport to the gate agent, I recognize that this would not be her kind of travel. We wouldn't be visiting museums filled with art or eating gourmet meals. Instead we will stay in a simple hostel and dine on tortillas, rice and beans. In this beautiful country, poverty is rampant. Many of the people we meet barely have enough to survive and yet each time I get off the plane in Managua, I am filled with uncontrollable joy. There is a richness here that defies logic, a warmth in the people and a generosity that is palpable.

I stand on the porch of a house in El Progresso, a small community in the mountains just outside Matagalpa and close my eyes to listen. A gentle wind blows in the banana trees and the joyful sound of children's voices dance all around us. In the distance I hear a bell jingling. I breathe in the cool mountain air and for the first time in many months, I notice that the knot in my stomach I have been feeling ever since my mother's death, is gone.

We have come to see a small school just up the hill and to learn about life in this mountain community. A man, a little over 5 feet tall, steps onto the porch. His blue striped shirt is stretched and stained and the oversized khaki green pants he wears are tucked into his rain boots and look as if they were intended for someone else. "This is Don Eric," our guide tells the students, "This is his house. You are his guests."

Don Eric spoke softly. "Bienvenidos," he said. "Gracias por su visita." *Thank you for your visit.* A year ago, he tells us, the porch where we stand was filled with children. The school up the hill was too small for the 75 preschoolers who live in this community and so, Don Eric and his wife Sandra, offered their home to be used as a preschool.

The porch is small, no more than 5 feet wide and twice as long and surrounded by flowers. Purple spidery cleome and deep pink celosia. A spikey lemon-colored flower caught my eye. "Qué tipo de flor es esto?" I asked. *What type of flower is this?* But I do not understand his answer. The dirt floor was etched with footprints of people who have come and gone in the past few days. Laundry lines filled with clothes ran two and three deep, the length of the small adobe house. A white board, a remnant from the days when this was a classroom, still hung in the corner. The family dog, a skinny white and brown mix, lay patiently in her small bed while her five puppies suckled. Inside the house, a baby slept in a hammock strung from the ceiling, seemingly unaware of the 17 gringos who had just come to visit.

As half the group stepped into Don Eric's small kitchen for a lesson in tortilla making, I wandered down the dirt road and landed in a forest of banana, coffee and lime trees. I felt like Alice in Wonderland, so small in their company. The large red flower of the banana tree announced the arrival of another cluster of fruit. Marlon, one of the nicaragüense who have escorted us up to the mountain, reaches up and pulls down a small green limón dulce from a nearby tree. He scratches the skin with his thumbnail and hands it to me to smell. The odor was fragrant, bright and acidy. He hands me another. A different type this time. This one is slightly smaller, more yellow in color than green. Again he pierces the skin with his thumbnail and I press it to my nose. He points out a cluster of small green bananas hanging from a tree. "Manzano," I repeated in Spanish. There are so many varieties of fruit I can barely keep them straight.

In all the travel I'd done over the years, I've never seen anything like rural Nicaragua. The majestic mountains, lush vegetation, and peaceful country lifestyle contrast dramatically with the frenetic pace of the city of Matagalpa. Inside the city cars whizz by. Horns honk tirelessly. Small fruit stands line the narrow streets and there are people everywhere. There are no museums to visit. No cathedrals to explore. It is raw, coarse and electric.

Inside the small dark kitchen, Sandra, Don Eric's wife, holds up two small plastic bowls of corn to show us. Maize seco, the dried corn, rattled in the base of the small yellow bowl. In the other is corn that has been boiled in lime and water until it softens and is ready to grind. Water, precious water. There are no faucets in this kitchen. The water has been collected from the summer rains in a cistern at the back of Don Eric's house.

Sandra pours the soaked corn into the top of the small steel mill that is clamped to her rough wood plank counter and motions me forward. I leaned into the work, using my body weight to turn the stiff crank with a herky jerky motion. In a handmade wooden crib that sits in the corner, Sandra's youngest, a beautiful baby boy with a round face and gentle brown eyes, looked on as I struggled. I turn over the work to one of the students. Round and round and round we go until all eight of us take a turn but we are not finished.

"Uno vez más," she says, *One more time.* She feeds the ground corn back into the grinder. The grind is too rough to cook with after one turning. It must be ground again.

I start again, and then, when my arm was tired, I motion to Nick, a tall young man with disheveled brown hair, green eyes and a James Dean type smile, one of the two young men in our group. He turned and turned until all the corn passes through.

Sandra puts a few gently used circles of wax paper down on the small, wooden table. The table is unsteady on the uneven dirt floor. She grabs a handful of the ground corn masa and shapes it into a small ball, the size of the limón dulce now tucked in my pocket. Flattening it with the palm of her hand, she shows us how to shape a tortilla, patting the dough with a flat hand and turning it with the other until it makes a perfectly round circle. Peeling it from the paper, she places it on a hot pan that sits atop a small adobe stove in the corner of the room. Feeding the fire from below, she pokes at the wood until she is happy with the flame. The thick black smoke from the fire flows up the chimney and out into the cool mountain air. I am struck by how unusual this is. Most of the homes we have been to have no chimney. The smoke stays in the kitchen and sticks to the walls, painting the inside of the house with a thick black layer of soot.

One by one we take turns shaping a tortilla. While we work, a small brown pig scampers across the kitchen floor and burrows himself under one of the half a dozen plastic lawn chairs that have been set out for us. Laughter fills the room as each of us struggles to make even one that resembles the kind we've seen in the grocery store. Each morning Sandra rises at 5 a.m. to prepare the tortillas for the day. 24 perfectly round tortillas, made by hand for her family. She pulls our misshapen rounds from the fire, her fingers insensitive to the heat, and we fill them with beans and a few slices of avocado. "Qué rico," I said. *Delicious.* It is the best tortilla I have ever tasted.

I walked up the steep hill from Don Eric's house to the new school, a beautiful building made of red brick, recycled glass and concrete. I pause by a simple washstand made of corrugated tin, one of the original structures on the property. There is no running water, no spigot, just a small bucket of clean water for the children to wash their hands.

The classroom, kitchen and library were completed last year. The group steps inside the new building and squeezes into the tiny wooden desks that encircle the room. The desks squeak on the red tile floor as we settle in. I think about the child that sat in this very desk just that morning, dressed in a blue and white government issued uniform. I imagine the sound of her voice as she eagerly called to a classmate, her voice ringing with enthusiasm.

In the front of the room stands the woman we'd picked up along the road. She is one of two teachers at the school. Each morning, she walks 7 kilometers to teach her class. There are very few cars here, and during the summer rains, the unpaved road to the community is often impassable. A few minutes later one of her students enters through the wooden door and takes her place in the front of the class. She will recite a poem, the teacher tells us. A poem by Rubén Darío, who is a hero in these parts. "Qué alegre y fresca la mañanita!" *How happy and fresh the early morning.* The poem, "Del Trópico" comes pouring out of her mouth as she twists and turns in front of us, her hands moving in harmony with every syllable.

As I look around the room, it is easy to understand why Don Eric calls the new school "a temple". Sunlight streams through the stained glass window, a window made of recycled bottles. One of the students runs his hand across the surface of a dozen or more cut bottles that have been cemented into place. "I put these here," he says, as his voice trails off. Nick was part of a group who worked on this building the past year.

Earlier in the morning while we were at the worksite, I stood in the hot sun, laying bricks. The worksite was abuzz with people. A group of students turned shovels of concrete, sand and water to make mezcla, the mix that we use to secure the brick as we build the walls of the new classroom. Community members, mostly women in tattered skirts and flip flops, haul buckets of rock that will be used to level the ground and build a retaining wall. The children, on a break from class, buzz in and out of the work site like hummingbirds. The air is thick and sweat drips in my eyes and soaks my clothes.

"Agua," the foreman interrupts, *Drink some water.* "Estás cansada?" *Are you tired?*

"No," I say and clap my hands together, releasing the thick gooey mezcla from my gloves. I bend down and pick up another brick, slathering the mezcla on the wall like peanut butter on a slice of bread. Here, far away from home, I am happy. I do not want to stop.

As I lay bricks, a young woman dressed in a worn purple jacket and blue jeans stood beside me. Chatting away in Spanish, she peppers me with dozens of questions before I finally recognize one I could answer. "Como se llama?" she asks. *What is your name?*

"Susanna, soy profesora de los estudiantes. *I am the teacher of the students.* "Y tu?"

"Marisela," she said. She is 16 and no longer in school. She lives in the community with her siblings. Her mother died this past October, she says, at the age of 47.

"47?" I repeated, not sure I understood her correctly.

"Si."

"Lo siento," I say. *I am sorry.* "Ella era muy joven." *She was very young.* I pause for a moment, and then, "Mi madre murió también, el año pasado, en Enero." *My mother died too, last year, in January.* For a moment the conversation between us stops. "Es muy difícil," I say in Spanish. *It is very hard.* She too is an orphan. For a moment we lock eyes and then she tells me about her mother through her tears. I wish I knew enough Spanish to tell her about mine.

What would I have said? What could I have said? When I was still slogging through the aftermath of my mother's death, mired in the weeds of the many decisions that followed her passing? As I continued to sort through my memories, trying to decide what to keep and what to let go? What might I have said about a mother I still did not understand?

I did not know back then, but now, more than two years later, I do. I would tell her that my mother was a star whose light shown brightly. She was smart and witty and enormously talented. I would tell her that she loved her children passionately and that she worked hard to give us the life she dreamed for us. That she exposed us to literature and culture. That she lectured us on the importance of a strong connection to our family. I would tell her that my mother gave me the gift of education and taught me the importance of travel. She showed me that gathering around the table and sharing a meal is a way to offer love and that baseball is about so much more than the final score. And although she would not live to see them grow into the men they would eventually become, my children will always know that their Nana loved them.

But for everything she gave me, she could not give me the one thing I desperately wanted, the kind of relationship I always hoped for. She could not see me for who I was, only who she wanted me to be. She could not be honest with me or allow me to be honest with her. Honesty requires the willingness to know that we don't know. To listen when we don't understand.

To sit in the questions. Honesty requires vulnerability and my mother could not be vulnerable.

It has taken me a long time to realize that it was never a zero sum choice. My mother convinced us it was. I grew up believing that to love and honor her meant that I needed to protect her at all costs and in doing so deny a part of myself. I believed that I could not speak my truth for fear of disappointing her. I believed that I could only belong to the family if I followed her rules and I wanted so desperately to belong. And so I built walls to protect myself and armored myself with anger.

But now I understand that two things can be equally true. Although the anger protected me, it kept me from showing her the person I so desperately wanted her to see. I will never know what might have occurred if I had spoken up. If I had challenged the family rules. Like a good daughter I stayed in her shadow, but now I understand it needn't have been that way. I could love and honor her and still speak my truth. It wasn't either/or. It could be both/and.

I wonder what might have happened if I had not given up. How might it have shaped my relationship with her? With my father? With my siblings? How would it have affected our family system? How might it have changed me? In the end I have learned what I already knew to be true, what over 30 years in social work has taught me, that at the heart of our very existence is connection. That true connection is the thing we all desire. It is what makes us human. The thing I most wanted and the only thing that matters. Connection is what heals all of us.

But it was not to be. I have come to understand that my mother did the best she could. It has taken me a long time to accept that. It wasn't that she didn't want to give me what I needed. She couldn't. She just couldn't.

Alzheimer's did not erase my mother. Now, when I look in the mirror, it is her face I see. But there is also another reflection. The reflection of a woman who found her way. Who has learned to love her family and herself. Who has realized that we live on in each other. My mother in me. Me in my children. It is the connection that will not be denied.

It is the *we* in me. The *we* in all of us.

On our last night in Nicaragua, we gathered to say goodbye. In the morning we would board a plane back to San Francisco, back to the world we escaped just a week before. Around the room, the faces of my students looked sunburned and tired, but the sound of their voices is electric. We took turns saying goodbye.

As we shared what we were grateful for, we tossed a ball of yarn from one person to the next, each holding on to the string as we pass it to another. Choking back tears, I told the students I was grateful for their hard work and generosity. I passed the yarn ball to Molly, one of my students. Molly had cerebral palsy and walked with a cane. She thanked the group for helping her. During the week they stood by her navigating the unpredictable landscape. Without ramps or elevators or motorized carts, she relied on kindness paired with determination, grit and a positive attitude.

"We left San Francisco as strangers," she said as tears streamed down her face. "But now you are my family."

In the end we created a brightly colored spider web, a symbol of the connections we'd made that week. We took a pair of scissors and cut the yarn into pieces, each taking a piece to remember our time together. I went back to my room and lay down on the bed but I could not sleep. I tossed and turned for a while and then sat up. I turned on the small bedside lamp and reached for the scrap of yarn. I tied it around my wrist and turned off the light.

# *Acknowledgements*

When my mother developed Alzheimer's disease, I longed to find a way to hold on to her, to keep her from disappearing. I knew she would not see my children graduate from college or marry or have children. I wanted to make sure they remembered her and so, I began to do the only thing I could think of, to do what she had taught me to do. I began to write. I started and stopped, started and stopped again. I got lost and turned around. I struggled to find a path in, a way to capture the woman I had spent my whole life trying to understand but the words would not come. She remained as she had always been, larger than life. And so I did something that has always been very hard for me. I asked for help.

I am forever grateful to Elaine Silver, my intuitive and wholehearted content editor and coach who held my feet to the fire and provided a flashlight for me when the path seemed dark. To my brother Robert, who encouraged me and served as my sounding board through this difficult and wonderful journey. To my husband, Bob, who gave me the space and support I needed to dive deep into my memories and make this dream come true. To Frances Rivetti, Catherine Barden and Ashley Kelly, whose early feedback strengthened and clarified my vision. To Stevan Nikolic and Adelaide Books for helping me bring this story into the world. To Sara Rosalsky who spent hours working to restore an old family photo for the cover. To my parents, Thomas and Beatrice Maggio and to my brothers and sister who taught me the importance of family. And finally, to my children whose love for their Nana allowed me to see her in a different way. This story is for you.

# About the Author

Throughout her 30 year career as a licensed clinical social worker, Suzanne Maggio has helped hundreds of families improve their relationships by encouraging them to open their hearts and share their stories. She now trains the new generation of helpers as a university lecturer in Psychology, Counseling and Social Work. The granddaughter of Italian immigrants, she grew up understanding the importance of family and the pleasures of gathering around a dining room table laden with good company and delicious food. Passionate about travel, cooking and sports, Suzanne is an avid baseball fan. She attended her first New York Mets baseball game at the age of eight with her grandfather, a former sports writer from Italy. In 2016 she won a silver award from Travelers Tales for "Yo Soy," a story about the search for identity while traveling in Nicaragua. Her work has been published in Sonoma Family Life, an award winning parenting magazine and Junior Baseball Magazine.

She lives in Northern California with her husband, where they raised their two sons and where they now manage three rambunctious dogs and a brood of demanding chickens.

Printed in Great Britain
by Amazon